American Book Company's

MASTERING THE GEORGIA

6TH GRADE

CRCT

IN

ENGLISH LANGUAGE ARTS

Rob Hunter
Kristie White

Contributing Writers:
Jason Kirk
Leah Ott
Moss Hall
Project Coordinator: Zuzana Urbanek
Executive Editor: Dr. Frank Pintozzi

American Book Company
PO Box 2638
Woodstock, GA 30188-1383
Toll Free: 1 (888) 264-5877   Phone: (770) 928-2834
Fax: (770) 928-7483   Toll Free Fax: 1 (866) 827-3240
www.americanbookcompany.com

ACKNOWLEDGEMENTS

The authors would like to gratefully acknowledge the editing and technical contributions of Marsha Torrens and Yvonne Benson. In addition, the authors wish to thank Peggy Keenum for her writing contributions.

We also want to thank and Rachae Brooks for developing the graphics for this book.

A special thanks to Charisse Johnson for the original icon.

The image on page 187 reprinted courtesy The Oyez Project

ALL RIGHTS RESERVED

Table of Contents

PREFACE

Mastering the Georgia 6th Grade CRCT in English Language Arts will help students who are learning or reviewing material for the CRCT. The materials in this book are based on the GPS standards as published by the Georgia Department of Education. This book is written to the grade 6 reading level, corresponding to approximately 850L to 1050L on the Lexile text measure scale.

This book contains several sections. These sections are as follows: 1) general information about the book; 2) a diagnostic test; 3) an evaluation chart; 4) chapters that teach the concepts and skills that improve CRCT readiness; 5) two practice tests. Answers to the tests and exercises are in a separate manual. The answer manual also contains a chart of standards for teachers to make a more precise diagnosis of student needs and assignments and a section of activities for extension and differentiation. This book is written to the grade 6 reading level, corresponding to approximately 850L to 1050L on the Lexile text measure scale.

We welcome comments and suggestions about the book. Please contact us at

American Book Company
PO Box 2638
Woodstock, GA 30188-1383

Toll Free: 1 (888) 264-5877
Phone: (770) 928-2834
Fax: (770) 928-7483
Web site: www.americanbookcompany.com

About the Authors

Rob Hunter is Copy Editor and ELA Writer at American Book Company. He has more than 10 years of experience teaching grammar, reading, English composition, and other subjects to students at various levels. He graduated from Georgia State University in 1995 with a Bachelor of Arts in English.

Kristie White is a language arts teacher in the Georgia Public School System. Since 2000, she has taught a variety of language arts and English courses ranging from the middle grades through the college level. Her Ed.S. degree is from Mercer University.

About the Project Coordinator: Zuzana Urbanek serves as ELA Curriculum Coordinator for American Book Company. She is a professional writer with 25 years of experience in education, business, and publishing. She has taught a variety of English courses since 1990 at the college level and also taught English as a foreign language abroad. Her master's degree is from Arizona State University.

About the Executive Editor: Dr. Frank J. Pintozzi is a former Professor of Education at Kennesaw (GA) State University. For over 28 years, he has taught English and reading at the high school and college levels as well as in teacher preparation courses in language arts and social studies. In addition to writing and editing state standard-specific texts for high school exit and end of course exams, he has edited and written numerous college textbooks.

TEST-TAKING TIPS

1. Complete the chapters and practice tests in this book. This text will help you review the skills for the CRCT in English Language Arts.

2. Be prepared. Get a good night's sleep the day before your exam. Eat a well-balanced meal, one that contains plenty of proteins and carbohydrates, prior to your exam.

3. Arrive early. Allow yourself at least 15–20 minutes to find your room and get settled. Then you can relax before the exam, so you won't feel rushed.

4. Think success. Keep your thoughts positive. Turn negative thoughts into positive ones. Tell yourself you will do well on the exam.

5. Practice relaxation techniques. Some students become overly worried about exams. Before or during the test, they may perspire heavily, experience an upset stomach, or have shortness of breath. If you feel any of these symptoms, talk to a close friend or see a counselor. They will suggest ways to deal with test anxiety. Here are some quick ways to relieve test anxiety:
   - Imagine yourself in your most favorite place. Let yourself sit there and relax.
   - Do a body scan. Tense and relax each part of your body starting with your toes and ending with your forehead.
   - Use the 3-12-6 method of relaxation when you feel stress. Inhale slowly for three seconds. Hold your breath for twelve seconds, and then exhale slowly for six seconds.

6. Read directions carefully. If you don't understand them, ask the proctor for further explanation before the exam starts.

7. Use your best approach for answering the questions. Some test-takers like to skim the questions and answers before reading the problem or passage. Others prefer to work the problem or read the passage before looking at the answers. Decide which approach works best for you.

8. Answer each question on the exam. Unless you are instructed not to, make sure you answer every question. If you are not sure of an answer, take an educated guess. Eliminate choices that are definitely wrong, and then choose from the remaining answers.

9. Use your answer sheet correctly. Make sure the number on your question matches the number on your answer sheet. In this way, you will record your answers correctly. If you need to change your answer, erase it completely. Smudges or stray marks may affect the grading of your exams, particularly if they are scored by a computer. If your answers are on a computerized grading sheet, make sure the answers are dark. The computerized scanner may skip over answers that are too light.

10. Check your answers. Review your exam to make sure you have chosen the best responses. Change answers only if you are sure they are wrong.

Georgia 6th Grade CRCT in English Language Arts Diagnostic Test

The purpose of this diagnostic test is to measure your reading and writing skills. This diagnostic test is based on the GPS-based CRCT standards for English Language Arts and adheres to the sample question format provided by the Georgia Department of Education.

General Directions:

1. Read all directions carefully.

2. Read each question or sample. Then choose the best answer.

3. Choose only one answer for each question. If you change an answer, be sure to erase your original answer completely.

4. After taking the test, you or your instructor should score it using the evaluation chart following the test. This will enable you to determine your strengths and weaknesses. Then study chapters in this book corresponding to topics that you need to review.

Note: The corresponding GPS standards listed beside each question have the prefix "ELA" removed to make the best use of space.

1 **What type of noun is the underlined word?** 6C1a.i

"Kindness is one of your best qualities," Charlene's mother said to her.

A abstract noun

B proper noun

C possessive noun

D plural noun

2 **What type of pronoun is the underlined word?** 6C1a.ii

Jeremy wonders if <u>that</u> is the right answer to his math question.

A personal

B possessive

C reflexive

D demonstrative

3 **What type of adjective is the underlined word?** 6C1a.iii

The <u>Hawks</u> basketball that was signed by the high scorer was auctioned for charity.

A common

B proper

C demonstrative

D indefinite

4 **What type of verb is the underlined word?** 6C1a.iv

When the class was studying Spanish, they all <u>cooked</u> tortillas.

A transitive

B intransitive

C linking

D helping

5 **What type of verb is the underlined group of words?** 6C1a.v

Isabelle <u>has been</u> painting a miniature house with all its furniture.

A linking

B state-of-being

C helping

D action

6 **What part of speech is the underlined word?** 6C1a.vi

The traffic on the tree-lined street has become <u>exceedingly</u> heavy.

A a preposition

B an adverb

C an adjective

D a verb

7 **Which word in the sentence is a preposition?** 6C1a.vii

Kyle and Austin were going to the movies together on Saturday.

A going

B to

C together

D Saturday

8 **Which word in the sentence is a coordinating conjunction?** 6C1a.viii

Sarah and Samantha like to meet at the bookstore to see what new books have arrived.

A and

B like

C meet

D what

9 **Where should quotation marks be placed in the sentence?** 6C1f 6W2 6W4c

The flight attendant said, The seat belt sign has been turned on by our pilot.

A before *flight* and after *attendant*

B before *attendant* and after *sign*

C before *The* and after *turned*

D before *The* and after *pilot*

10 **What part of speech is the underlined word?** 6C1a.ix

Hey! What are you doing with all those basketballs on the sidewalk?

A noun

B pronoun

C adverb

D interjection

11 **Which word in the sentence is the simple subject?** 6C1b

Having been a sports fan all his life, Joaquin was thrilled to become a first-round draft choice in the NFL.

A fan

B life

C Joaquin

D choice

12 **Which type of sentence is the sentence below?** 6C1c

My favorite television program is about cooking, and my sister's favorite program is about decorating.

A a simple sentence

B a complex sentence

C a compound sentence

D a complex-compound sentence

13 **Which sentence uses the semicolon correctly?** 6C1d

A Many people are running late today; because the traffic light was broken.

B Click on the computer icon on your desktop; it will show you the CD player.

C Whether we want to or not; studying helps us become better students.

D There are more than fifty horses running; around in the field.

14 **Which word in the sentence is spelled incorrectly?** 6C1e,f 6W2 6W4c

The military patrolman did not dessert his post while he was on duty.

A military

B dessert

C post

D while

15 Where should the comma be placed in the sentence? 6C1f 6W2 6W4c

The class wants to take burgers fries, soft drinks, and ice cream on their picnic.

A after *wants*

B after *burgers*

C after *soft*

D after *cream*

16 Imagine that you want a friend to meet you at the library, but your friend does not know how to get there. Which organizational pattern would work BEST for the directions you need to write? 6W1a,c 6W2

A chronological

B cause-effect

C compare/contrast

D question-answer

Use the paragraph below to answer question 17.

Sometimes it seems like homework takes up more time than anything else in your life. Why do we students have to do so much homework? It helps us learn the lessons we hear about in school. It's one thing to have a teacher tell us something, but when we have to work it out on our own, that's when it really sinks in. So, next time you are facing hours of homework, look at it as the best way to learn—by doing!

17 What is the BEST evidence that this paragraph uses a question and answer pattern? 6W1a,c 6W2

A use of the transition *Why*

B use of the transition *but*

C use of the transition *So*

D use of an inverted sentence

18 Which word BEST fills the blank? 6W1d 6W4b

Mom and I planted some carrot seeds in a window-sill garden. We watered the garden and waited. _____, little green sprouts poked up through the soil.

A Until

B Finally

C So

D Although

Use the paragraph below to answer question 19.

1 My brother Troy is always pulling practical jokes. 2 The other day, my friend Lashon got him back with a really funny trick. 3 She had gotten permission to spend the night at my house. 4 First, she switched around everything on his desk. 5 He was confused because he's used to knowing where he keeps things. 6 Even funnier was that he couldn't answer his phone. 7 When it rang, he picked it up and said, "Hello? Hello?" but it kept on ringing because she had taped down the little plastic button that pops up when you answer a call. 8 It was hilarious!

19 **Which sentence does not relate to the rest of the paragraph and should be removed?**   6W2 6W4b

   A sentence 1

   B sentence 3

   C sentence 4

   D sentence 6

Use the paragraph below to answer question 20.

Last season, the Tidwell Tigers were at the top of their game. The team made it all the way to the regional finals. This year, let's cheer on our heroes to the finish line.

20 **Which sentence would be the BEST closing sentence for this paragraph?**   6W2 6W4b

   A We want to see the Tigers win it all!

   B Can the Tigers do as well as last year?

   C They made it quite far against worthy opponents.

   D The Tigers may not do as well this year.

Use the paragraph below to answer question 21.

The moon is close to the earth, so it has a direct effect on ocean tides. The tide rises on the side of the earth where the moon is, pulling at our gravity. The push and pull of the moon circling the earth raises and lowers tides. However, the moon is moving about an inch and a half away from the earth each year. Once it moves another 14,600 miles, it will be too far to influence the tides any longer.

21 **What is the main idea of this paragraph?**   6W2

   A The moon will influence ocean tides on earth as long as it stays close to the earth.

   B The gravitation push and pull is making the moon move farther away from the earth.

   C Soon, the moon will move away from the earth, and we will no longer be able to see it.

   D Earth's tides depend on the moon, so we need to find a way to keep it close to us.

Use the paragraph below to answer question 22.

There are elephants, chimpanzees, and even dolphins that paint. Zoos and aquariums encourage animal artists. It seems to help them cope with being penned up. Now, many animal lovers are paying big dollars for the artwork.

22 Which sentence would make the BEST topic sentence for this paragraph?   6W2

A Besides food, zoos buy art supplies for all their animals.

B Humans are not the only artists— some animals like to be creative.

C Did you know there's something new going on in zoos?

D In addition to animal care and feeding, zoo keepers need to keep animals mentally active.

Use the paragraph below to answer question 23.

1 It was the first time Mom and Dad let me stay home alone. **2** They were gone for only a couple of hours to pick up our new couch. **3** It was the scariest night of my life! **4** I thought I saw someone peeking in the window, and I heard noises! **5** When they got home, my parents explained they had asked the neighbor to peek in on me, and the noises were just the refrigerator and the hot water heater turning on. **6** I didn't care what the reasons were…I didn't want them to leave me alone again!

23 Which sentence is the topic sentence of the paragraph?   6W2

A sentence 1

B sentence 2

C sentence 3

D sentence 4

Use the paragraph below to answer question 24.

1 My mom is doing her annual spring cleaning. **2** She likes to listen to music while she cleans. **3** I asked her why spring cleaning is different from cleaning at any other time. **4** She explained that, in the winter, the house is all shut up. **5** Germs and stale air accumulate. **6** Spring is a great time to open windows, let in the fresh breeze, and air out things like blankets, cushions, and mattresses.

24 Which sentence does not relate to the rest of the paragraph and should be removed?   6W2 6W4b

A sentence 2

B sentence 3

C sentence 5

D sentence 6

Use the paragraph below to answer question 25.

1 My sister and I love playing video games. **2** Video games are fast and colorful, but sometimes a calmer, quieter game is good. **3** Now and then, it's fun to play board games. **4** My favorite board game is backgammon. **5** Usually, we have to pick something else, so neither of us constantly wins. **6** Jenny is a good speller, so she likes Scrabble.

25 In the paragraph above, sentence 6 is out of order. Where should it BEST be placed?   6W2 6W4b

A after sentence 1

B after sentence 2

C after sentence 3

D after sentence 4

Use the paragraph below to answer question 26.

Getting ready for school the night before can save you a lot of headaches. Try packing your book bag before you go to bed. Then, in the morning, you don't have to think about as much. It's hard to consider what you need that day when you have just woken up.

26 **Which sentence would be the BEST closing sentence for this paragraph?** 6W2 6W4b

A Have one of your parents make a list for you.

B It's much easier to get ready the previous night.

C Don't forget your lunch on the way out the door.

D One thing you can't pack ahead is your lunch.

27 **Which would be the BEST way to find information for a report about marine mammals?** 6W3a

A email a friend

B enter the keywords *marine mammals* into an Internet search engine

C post a question on the electronic bulletin board of the nearest aquarium

D search the library's database for books about fish

28 **What punctuation mark should be placed after the word *system*?** 6C1f 6W2 6W4c

Tyler's project was about all the planets in our solar system Mercury, Venus, Earth, Mars, Jupiter, Saturn, Uranus, and Pluto.

A a comma

B a period

C a colon

D a semicolon

29 **What type of noun is the underlined word?** 6C1a

Everyone on the basketball <u>team</u> went out to Pizza Hut after the game.

A abstract noun

B common noun

C possessive noun

D collective noun

30 **What type of pronoun is the underlined word?** 6C1aii

The language arts teacher asked, "<u>Who</u> is going to enter the Poetry Contest this year?"

A personal

B interrogative

C demonstrative

D possessive

31 **What word in the sentence is a demonstrative adjective?** 6C1a.iii

Having been to many concerts, Jessica decided that group was her favorite.

A many   C that

B concerts   D favorite

32 **Which word in the sentence is a linking verb?** 6C1a.iv

The moth becomes a beautiful butterfly in its last stage of development.

A becomes

B beautiful

C stage

D development

33 **Which word in the sentence is the object of a preposition?** 6C1a.vii

At the theater is a great movie for all adventure lovers.

A At C movie

B theater D adventure

34 **What type of conjunction is the underlined group of words?** 6C1a.viii

<u>Neither</u> Brittany <u>nor</u> Ashley wanted to spend the night in the backyard.

A common

B coordinating

C correlative

D subordinate

35 **Which sentence contains a predicate noun?** 6C1b

A Musicians are people who love to listen to music.

B Scientists are curious about the tiniest particles in the universe.

C Training for a marathon requires many hours of running.

D A dozen donuts mysteriously appeared on the kitchen table.

36 **What group of words is a sentence fragment?** 6C1c

A Courtney ran to the store.

B Jordan is wanting a new bike.

C Zachary can't wait for Christmas.

D Jasmine and her friends from school.

37 **Where should the comma be placed in the sentence?** 6C1c,d,f 6W2 6W4c

According to the principal our class was the best-behaved class in the auditorium.

A after *According*

B after *principal*

C after *class*

D after *best-behaved*

38 **Which word in the sentence is spelled incorrectly?** 6C1e,f 6W2 6W4c

Please except my apologies for bringing the wrong kind of dessert to the party.

A except

B bringing

C kind

D dessert

39 **Which word in the sentence should be capitalized?** 6C1f 6W2 6W4c

Many famous people, such as oprah Winfrey, live and work in Chicago, Illinois.

A people

B oprah

C live

D work

40 Which word BEST completes this sentence? 6W1d 6W4b

Jenny wanted to buy a t-shirt, _____ she realized she had forgotten her money at home.

A but

B while

C and

D for

Read this passage, and then answer question 41.

1 There are few trees in the city. 2 We need more trees for cleaner air. 3 The Urban Improvement Group is having a special tree-planting party next week. 4 We're going to attend and help plant trees!

41 Which transition BEST fits before sentence 3? 6W1d 6W4b

A. In other words,

B Because,

C Since,

D Therefore,

Use the paragraph below to answer question 42.

1 Concert tickets today can be very expensive. 2 It can take them months or years to recover from spending that money. 3 Many parents can't afford to take kids to see their favorite music stars. 4 Not wanting to miss out, some families take out loans or sell important household goods just to attend a special concert. 5 Is it really worth it?

42 In the paragraph above, sentence 2 is out of order. Where should it BEST be placed? 6W2 6W4b

A before sentence 1

B after sentence 3

C after sentence 4

D after sentence 5

Use the paragraph below to answer question 43.

1 In English class, we talked about writing books. 2 My choice was a book about airplanes because they have always fascinated me. 3 Miss Gresham asked us what kind of book we'd want to write if we became authors. 4 My book could be about planes for different purposes. 5 It could also include the history of flying. 6 I think people would enjoy reading my book.

43 In the paragraph above, sentence 3 is out of order. Where should it BEST be placed? 6W2 6W4b

A before sentence 1

B after sentence 1

C after sentence 4

D after sentence 5

44 **Which word BEST fills the blank?** 6W1d
6W4b

The average monthly rainfall is two inches. _____ it has not rained for three months, we're six inches short.

A Even though

B In addition

C Since

D Then

Use the paragraph below to answer question 45.

Do you think the school plays are just for the nerds? If you think they are, you could not be more wrong. Being in plays actually promotes some important skills. To act well, a person has to use memory to recall lines. But it doesn't stop there. Those lines have to be recited with the proper emotion, which exercises empathy. Finally, the words and actions have to happen in the moment and look natural. This means an actor has to watch and listen carefully. These are important skills for life, not just for the stage.

45 **What is the main idea of this paragraph?** 6W2

A Everyone should learn to act.

B Being in a school play will make you popular.

C Learning lines from a script exercises your brain.

D Acting promotes several important skills.

Use the paragraph below to answer question 46.

1 Do you really have to do your very best on every quiz and all assignments? 2 Well, it all adds up. 3 If you make better grades on everything you do, you will be more successful overall in school. 4 If you figure that this quiz or that paper is not important, you might suddenly have several bad grades in a row. 5 After all, you don't want to have to go to summer school, do you?

46 **Which sentence is the topic sentence of the paragraph?** 6W2

A sentence 1

B sentence 2

C sentence 3

D sentence 4

Use the paragraph below to answer question 47.

Many kids today are overweight. When that happens, they can have health problems. In addition, being overweight makes it harder to perform physical activities. Schools are trying to help by offering healthy and nutritious food choices. In the end, though, it's up to each individual to eat right and get exercise.

47 **Which sentence would make the BEST topic sentence for this paragraph?** 6W2

A Kids need to watch what they eat.

B Young people don't usually have weight problems.

C Lack of exercise is a major reason why so many people are overweight.

D Vending machines contain many unhealthy things to snack on.

Use the paragraph below to answer question 48.

1 When my friend Rogelio and I play video games, he goes on the cheat sites to see how to win. 2 I think that defeats the purpose. 3 It's fun to try to solve the puzzles and get through the challenges. 4 Rogelio doesn't get to have that fun because the cheat sites tell him what to do. 5 I still like going to his house, though, because his mom bakes the best cookies.

48 **Which sentence does not relate to the rest of the paragraph and should be removed?**   6W2 6W4b

A sentence 2

B sentence 3

C sentence 4

D sentence 5

Use the paragraph below to answer question 49.

The Talbots have a rule at their house: no TV until homework is finished. At first, it seems like a harsh rule. What if there is something you really want to see, and you want to finish homework later? Gini Talbot says that this happens sometimes, but mostly she doesn't mind the rule.

49 **Which sentence would be the BEST closing sentence for this paragraph?**   6W2 6W4b

A The Talbots also make their kids eat everything on their plates.

B This makes it difficult to watch certain programs that come on early in the evening.

C Once she finishes her homework, she can relax more than if it were still waiting for her.

D She has often asked her parents to change the rule to a more lenient one.

50 **Which word BEST fills in the blank in the sentence below?**   6C1f 6W2 6W4c

_____ favorite aunt is taking her to see *The Lion, the Witch, and the Wardrobe*.

A Danielles'

B "Danielles"

C 'Danielles'

D Danielle's

51 What word in the sentence is a possessive noun? 6C1a.i

After the Super Bowl game the Falcon's locker room was filled with reporters.

A game

B Falcon's

C locker

D reporters

52 What type of pronoun is the underlined word? 6C1a.ii

"Is there <u>anyone</u> here who would like to go to the game with me?" asked the coach.

A personal

B interrogative

C demonstrative

D indefinite

53 Which word in the sentence is a state-of-being verb? 6C1a.iv

The closest planet to earth is one of my favorites.

A to

B is

C one

D of

54 Which word is the simple predicate in the sentence below? 6C1b

Olivia experimented in her science class by combining sodium and chloride to make salt.

A experimented

B science

C combining

D make

55 What type of sentence is the sentence below? 6C1c

Meteorologists usually try to make long-term predictions for the next week.

A simple sentence

B compound sentence

C complex sentence

D compound-complex sentence

56 Which word in the sentence is an adjective? 6C1a.iii

My little brother likes to follow me around the room.

A little

B follow

C around

D room

57 Which word in the sentence is spelled incorrectly? 6C1e,f 6W2 6W4c

We are going to visit Tallahassee, the capital of Florida, and see its capital building.

A visit

B Tallahassee

C capital (before *of Florida*)

D capital (before *building*)

58 What word in the sentence is the direct object? 6C1b

A weather report always contains the conditions of the weather at the time of the report.

A weather

B report

C conditions

D time

59 **What word in the sentences should be capitalized?**

6C1f
6W2
6W4c

Some of the states in the southeast are Georgia, Florida, South Carolina, and Alabama. Georgia is one state that is north of Florida.

A states

B southeast

C one

D north

60 **What punctuation mark should be placed in the sentence after the word *paint*?**

6C1c,d,f
6W2
6W4c

The supplies I needed for my project were poster board and paint they were easy to get at the drugstore.

A a comma

B an apostrophe

C a quotation mark

D a semicolon

EVALUATION CHART FOR GEORGIA 6TH GRADE CRCT IN ENGLISH LANGUAGE ARTS DIAGNOSTIC TEST

Directions: On the following chart, circle the question numbers that you answered incorrectly, and evaluate the results. These questions are based on the *Georgia Performance Standards (GPS) for 6th Grade English Language Arts*. Then turn to the appropriate chapters, read the explanations, and complete the exercises. Review other chapters as needed. Finally, complete the practice test(s) to assess your progress and further prepare you for the **Georgia 6th Grade CRCT in English Language Arts**.

Note: Some question numbers will appear under multiple chapters because those questions require demonstration of multiple skills.

Chapter	Question Number
Chapter 1: Capitalization	39, 59
Chapter 2: Punctuation	9, 13, 15, 28, 37, 50, 60
Chapter 3: Working with Verbs	4, 5, 32, 53
Chapter 4: Nouns and Pronouns	1, 2, 29, 30, 51, 52
Chapter 5: Adjectives and Adverbs	3, 6, 31, 56
Chapter 6: Prepositions, Conjunctions, and Interjections	7, 8, 10, 33, 34
Chapter 7: Sentence Structure	11, 35, 54, 58
Chapter 8: Fragments and Run-ons	12, 36, 37, 55, 60
Chapter 9: Spelling	14, 38, 57
Chapter 10: Purposes and Patterns	16, 17, 18, 40, 41, 44
Chapter 11: Working with Paragraphs	16, 17, 18, 19, 20, 21, 22, 23, 24, 25, 26, 40, 41, 42, 43, 44, 45, 46, 47, 48, 49
Chapter 12: Resource Materials	27

Chapter 1
Capitalization

This chapter addresses the following GPS-based CRCT standards:

ELA6C1	The student demonstrates understanding and control of the rules of the English language, realizing that usage involves the appropriate application of conventions and grammar in both written and spoken formats. The student
	f. Produces final drafts that demonstrate accurate spelling and the correct use of punctuation and capitalization.
ELA6W2	The student demonstrates competence in a variety of genres.
	The student produces **technical** writing that:
	d. Applies rules of Standard English.
ELA6W4	The student consistently uses the writing process to develop, revise, and evaluate writing. The student
	c. Edits to correct errors in spelling, punctuation, etc.

In this chapter, you will learn the rules of capitalization. You will learn how to capitalize proper nouns, proper adjectives, regions, titles, and more. You will have opportunities to apply these rules in various practice exercises. You will also be able to see the rules used in real-life settings.

WHY ARE SOME WORDS CAPITALIZED?

You may ask yourself, "How do I know when to capitalize and when not to capitalize?" At first glance, it may appear to be a mystery. How does your teacher decide whether to mark your paper wrong or right when it comes to capitalization? Well, it really is easy to understand, once you know the rules of capitalization. In this chapter, we will review these rules.

NOUNS

Nouns are divided into two general categories: common nouns and proper nouns.

Common nouns are general persons, places, things, or ideas. A common noun is not normally capitalized. A common noun is only capitalized when it begins a sentence or a direct quotation or when it is part of an official title.

> **Examples:** girl, cat, mountain, store, movie, soldier, and bank.

In contrast, **proper nouns** are specific names of people, places, things, or ideas. Proper nouns are capitalized.

> **Examples:** Melanie, Snowball, **Mt. Kilimanjaro**, **Macy's**, **Toy Story**,
> **General Eisenhower**, and **Bank of America**.

Proper nouns also include the names of historical events, historic and geographic periods, documents, days and months, holidays and religious days, and special events.

> **Examples:** the Renaissance, the Civil War, the Bill of Rights, Monday,
> December, Easter, Christmas, and the Super Bowl

Proper nouns further include the names of ships, trains, missiles, aircraft, spacecraft, monuments, memorials, buildings, awards, planets, and stars.

> **Examples:** *SS Titanic*, Lincoln Memorial, Fox Theater, Mars and Venus

Brand names and trade names should be considered proper nouns that are capitalized.

> **Examples:** Apple, Xerox, Chick-fil-A, and Ugg

The names of organizations, teams, businesses, institutions, government bodies, nationalities, races, and peoples are proper nouns that should be capitalized.

> **Examples:** Caucasian, Cherokee, and Asian

Sometimes proper nouns are formed from more than one word. In this case, prepositions and articles are not capitalized.

> **Examples:** Tomb of the Unknown Soldier and the University of Georgia

Practice 1: Nouns
6C1f, 6W4c

For each of question, choose the answer that best fills in the sentence using correct capitalization.

1. Take a hike up _____ C _____.

   A. the Mountain

   B. stone Mountain

   C. Stone Mountain

   D. Stone mountain

2. We went on ___D___.

   A. a campus visit to the University

   B. a campus visit to harvard

   C. a campus visit to Harvard university

   D. a campus visit to Harvard University

3. My parents decided to move us to ___A___.

   A. Gwinnett County

   B. Gwinnett county

   C. gwinnett County

   D. gwinnett county

4. My friends and I decided to raft down the
   ___A___.

   A. Chattahoochee River

   B. Chattahoochee river

   C. chattahoochee river

   D. chattahoochee River

5. Our class took a trip to see ___B___.

   A. america's Bill Of Rights

   B. America's Bill of Rights

   C. America's bill of Rights

   D. america's Bill of rights

6. In class, we read *The Firm* by ___D___.

   A. a famous Writer

   B. the Writer John Grisham

   C. the writer John grisham

   D. a famous writer

7. I have always wanted to ___B___.

   A. visit the eiffel tower

   B. visit the Eiffel Tower

   C. visit the Eiffel tower

   D. visit the eiffel Tower

8. In my history class we _____.
   A. discussed the conqueror alexander the Great
   B. discussed the conqueror Alexander the great
   C. discussed the conqueror Alexander The Great
   D. discussed the conqueror Alexander the Great

THE PRONOUN I AND BEGINNINGS OF SENTENCES

In English, **capitalize the pronoun I** as it refers to the speaker.

> **Example:** I went to the store yesterday to buy some milk.

Never write the pronoun I as a lower case letter.

Also, **always capitalize the first word of a sentence**.

> **Example:** Jumping up, I ran to the door.

Practice 2: The Pronoun I and Beginnings of Sentences
6C1f

In the sentences below, identify the choices that have errors in capitalization.

1. waterfalls and lightning storms are things that I always look at with awe.
   A. waterfalls   B. lightning   C. storms   D. I

2. Camping at Stone Mountain is an activity that i enjoy with my family.
   A. Camping   B. Mountain   C. i   D. family

3. My friends and I love to float down the chattahoochee River.
   A. My   B. I   C. chattahoochee   D. River

4. i hope to go hiking this summer with my dad and my brother Billy.
   A. i   B. summer   C. dad   D. Billy

PROPER ADJECTIVES

What is a **proper adjective**? Remember that an adjective is something that describes a noun or pronoun. It answers the questions *What kind?* and *Which one?* A proper adjective, then, is formed from a proper noun or is formed when a proper noun is used as an adjective.

> **Examples:** *French* exchange student, *Shakespearean* verse, the *Dark* Ages, and the *Revolutionary* Period

Here are some exceptions to remember:

Do NOT capitalize certain frequently used proper adjectives.

> **Examples:** china cabinet, french toast, and bowie knife

Capitalize a brand name used as a proper adjective but NOT the word it is describing

> **Examples:** Maytag refrigerator and Levi's jeans

Do NOT capitalize a common noun used with two or more adjectives

> **Examples:** Jackson, Bennet, and Morgan streets, and Seine and Nile rivers

Do NOT capitalize a prefix attached to a proper adjective unless it refers to a nationality.

> **Examples:** pro-English and Franco-Prussian War

In a hyphenated adjective, capitalize only the proper adjectives.

> **Examples:** French-speaking immigrant

Practice 3: Proper Adjectives
6C1f, 6W4c

Complete each sentence with the correct proper adjective.

1. In school, I decided to study the _____ *C* _____ language.
    A. Best   B. french   C. German   D. only

2. Jesse and Sarah go to the _____ *A* _____ church on Sundays.
    A. Methodist   B. catholic   C. better   D. worst

3. The local museum displayed art from the _____ *B* _____ culture.
    A. Lovely   B. Mayan   C. aztec   D. valued

4. Our class was able to study artwork from Picasso's _____ *C* _____ Period.
    A. Happiest   B. best   C. Cubist   D. blue

5. I like to eat _____ *C* _____ food on Friday nights.
    A. hot   B. foreign   C. Italian   D. mexican

6. I think that the most beautiful sounding accent is the _____ *B* _____ accent.
    A. France   B. Spanish   C. german   D. scottish

TITLES

What sorts of titles must be capitalized? This is an important question to know and understand.

First, make sure to capitalize **titles of people** when used with a proper name and as a name in a direct address.

- *With a proper name*: Yesterday President Carter spoke on his trade proposal.
- *As a name in a direct address*: Excuse me, Professor, Julie Allen is on hold for you.

> **Examples:** Sir, Madam, Doctor, Professor, Reverend, Rabbi, Sister, Senator, Governor, Archbishop, Mr., Mrs., Dr., Jr., Sr., Ph.D., Commander in Chief, and Secretary of Finance

Second, capitalize the **titles of family members** when they are used with a name or as a name.

> **Examples:** Did you know that Aunt Reba vacations in Barbados every year? I wish that Grandma would bake those cookies with the peanut butter cups in them. I am excited that Cousin Grace will be staying with us for the weekend.

Third, capitalize **titles of books, periodicals, poems, stories, historical documents, movies, art, television programs, and musical works**.

> **Examples:** *The Tragedy of Macbeth, The Giver, Ratatouille*, and *Sports Illustrated*

Fourth, capitalize the **titles of courses** when they are the name of a language or when they are followed by a number.

> **Examples:** Spanish, Chinese, Biology 101, and Zoology 245

Practice 4: Titles
6C1f, 6W4c

Read the following sentences. Pick the choice that is written correctly.

1. In my sister's first semester of college, she had to take the basic ____D____.

   A. english 101 class   C. english 101 Class

   B. English 101 Class   D. English 101 class

2. On ____A____, grandpa decided to watch the movie *Gone with the Wind*.

   A. Last saturday   C. last Saturday

   B. last saturday   D. Last Saturday

3. Yesterday, the ____B____ resigned from his position.

   A. governor of New York   C. Governor Of New York

   B. Governor of New York   D. governor of new york

4. Did you call ___*A*___ about that ear infection?
   A. Dr. Peterson
   B. dr. Peterson
   C. dr. peterson
   D. Dr. peterson

5. The president's visit to the city caused a huge traffic jam ___*C*___.
   A. on broad Street
   B. on broad street
   C. on Broad Street
   D. on Broad street

6. The student government supported Marisol as the ___*D*___.
   A. vice president
   B. Vice president
   C. vice President
   D. Vice President

PLACES

The **names of places** also must be capitalized. Places include continents, countries, cities, towns, counties, states, islands, bodies of water, streets/highways, parks/forest, mountains, and regions.

Examples: North America, France, Ireland, Conyers, Dacula, Georgia, Florida, Puerto Rico, Bahamas, Indian Ocean, Dead Sea, Broad Street, Amicalola State Park, Mount St. Helens, and the South.

Note: Be careful in using the directional words. Do not capitalize words that indicate a general direction. Do, however, capitalize words indicating a region.

Example: Drive north on I-75 until you reach Tennessee. (direction)

Example: I went to college in the Midwest. (region)

Note: In a hyphenated street number, only capitalize the first word.

Example: South Thirty-seventh Street

Practice 5:   Places
6C1f, 6W4c

Read each of the sentences below and pick the correct answer.

1. Oscar Wilde was a popular writer from ___*C*___.
   A. Dublin, ireland
   B. dublin, Ireland
   C. Dublin, Ireland
   D. dublin, ireland

2. We had to drive south on Main Street to find the entrance to
    __D__.

    A. darden park

    B. Darden park

    C. darden Park

    D. Darden Park

3. For Memorial Day, our family is hiking up Stone Mountain in __D__.

    A. dekalb county   C. dekalb County

    B. Dekalb county   D. Dekalb County

4. For my summer abroad, I traveled to __D__.

    A. france, germany, the Netherlands, and spain

    B. France, germany, the netherlands, and spain

    C. France, Germany, The Netherlands, and Spain

    D. France, Germany, the Netherlands, and Spain

CHAPTER 1 SUMMARY

Capitalize the **first word in a sentence**.

Capitalize the **pronoun I**.

Capitalize **proper nouns** and **proper adjectives**.

Capitalize the **names of people**.

Capitalize **geographical names**.

Capitalize **historical events, periods, special events**, and **calendar items**.

Don't Forget!

Capitalize the **names of nationalities, races, and people**.

Capitalize the **names of organizations, teams, businesses, institutions, and governments bodies**.

Capitalize **brand names**.

Capitalize **ships, monuments, awards**, and **planets**.

Capitalize **titles before and after names**.

Capitalize **words showing family relationship** when followed by a name.

Capitalize the **titles of books, movies, plays, stories, television programs, artwork, magazines, and historical documents**.

Capitalize **countries, states, continents, cities/towns, counties, islands, bodies of water, streets/highways, parks/forest, mountains**, and **regions**.

CHAPTER 1 REVIEW

6C1f, 6W4c

Part I: In the sentences below, identify the errors in capitalization.

1   The famous book *Quest for Tomorrow* that we read in English 102 was written by uncle Rick.

   A Quest for Tomorrow   **C** uncle Rick

   B English 102   **D** no error

2   I bought my Grandma a first edition copy of *Superman* for Christmas.

   A Grandma   **B** Superman   **C** Christmas   **D** no error

3   In Atlanta, the High Museum of Art is showing the art of the impressionist period for the month of June.

   A High Museum of Art

   B impressionist period

   C June

   D no error

4   I bought a box of kleenex because the movie *The Kite Runner* is supposed to be a tearjerker.

   A kleenex   **C** tearjerker

   B *The Kite Runner*   **D** no error

5   Jazz music is influenced by african and European music.

   A Jazz music   **C** European

   B african   **D** no error

6   The directions say to take Sixty-Ninth street west until it becomes Jackson Highway.

   A Sixty-Ninth street   **C** Jackson Highway

   B west   **D** no error

7   The national honor society requires all of its members to volunteer, so I worked at St. Mary's Catholic Church's food kitchen.

   A national honor society   **C** St. Mary's Catholic Church

   B I   **D** no error

8 Annie Leibovitz's work is often featured in *vogue* magazine and her own books of photography.

    A Annie Leibovitz   **C** photography

    B vogue   **D** no error

9 Next Monday, Mrs. Hallman's english class will celebrate St. Patrick's day with green jellybeans.

    A Monday   **C** jellybeans

    B english   **D** no error

10 Marla performed a creative dance while reciting the poem "O Captain! My Captain!" in the Booker T. Washington High School talent show.

    A "O Captain! My Captain!"

    B Booker T. Washington High School

    C creative dance

    D no error

Part II: Correct the capitalization errors in the letter below.

Dear mr. Pardee,

    1 After the speech you gave on the novel *The Outsiders*, I just had to read the book myself. **2** This story set in the west during the late 1960's spoke so strongly about the class struggles in teenagers' lives. **3** I was drawn into the world of Greasers and Socs, even though I am a samoan living in California. **4** I understood exactly what Ponyboy was living through. **5** I really connected with the themes of rejection, loss, belonging, judging, and misjudging because I see that they still exist today. **6** Thanks for speaking on those issues and bringing such a wonderful book to my attention.

Sincerely,

Paora ngaire

11 What correction should be made in the salutation?

A Don't capitalize *dear*.

B Capitalize *Mr.*

C Don't capitalize *Pardee*.

D No changes are needed.

12 What correction should be made in the first and second sentences of the body?

A Don't capitalize *The Outsiders*.

B Capitalize *west*.

C Capitalize *novel*.

D No changes are needed.

13 What correction should be made in the third and fourth sentences of the body?

A Don't capitalize *Greasers*.

B Don't capitalize *Socs*.

C Capitalize *samoan*.

D No changes are needed.

14 What correction should be made in the fifth and sixth sentences of the body?

A Capitalize *rejection*, *loss*, *belonging*, *judging*, and *misjudging*.

B Don't capitalize *I*.

C Capitalize *issues*.

D No changes are needed.

15 What correction should be made in the conclusion?

A Don't capitalize *Sincerely*.

B Don't capitalize *Paora*.

C Capitalize *ngaire*.

D No changes are needed.

Chapter 2
Punctuation

This chapter addresses the following GPS-based CRCT standards:

ELA6C1	The student demonstrates understanding and control of the rules of the English language, realizing that usage involves the appropriate application of conventions and grammar in both written and spoken formats. The student
	d. Demonstrates appropriate comma and semicolon usage (compound and complex sentences, appositives, words in direct address).
	f. Produces final drafts that demonstrate accurate spelling and the correct use of punctuation and capitalization.
ELA6W2	The student demonstrates competence in a variety of genres.
	The student produces **technical** writing (friendly letters, thank-you notes, formula poems, instructions) that:
	d. Applies rules of Standard English.
ELA6W4	The student consistently uses the writing process to develop, revise, and evaluate writing. The student
	c. Edits to correct errors in spelling, punctuation, etc.

Knowing how to punctuate correctly while writing is vitally important. Think of the confusion that would occur if nobody used correct punctuation! Punctuation helps the reader understand a piece of writing by organizing and clarifying ideas. In this chapter, you will review punctuation rules to make your writing more effective.

COMMAS

Use commas to separate items in a series.

> **Example:** My favorite foods are pizza, fries, ice cream, and blueberries. (words in a series)

> **Example:** On vacation, we went to the beach, played paintball, hiked up Stone Mountain, and rode roller coasters. (phrases in a series)

> **Example:** The artwork that Anna had struggled to create, that she carefully framed, and that she painstakingly hung was sold within two hours. (clauses in a series)

Note: Don't use commas if each item in a series is separated by *and* or *or*.

> **Example:** The cat hissed and clawed and scratched to get away.

Use commas to separate two or more adjectives describing a noun.

> **Example:** The dress is a soft, expensive material.

> **Example:** Danny is a smart, responsible, creative, energetic man.

Use commas after words like *well, yes, no,* and *why* when they begin a sentence.

> **Example:** Yes, we will be late for our meeting.

> **Example:** Well, you should hurry up.

Use a comma after an introductory phrase or clause.

> **Example:** Jumping up, Cory grabbed the dog before the door opened.

> **Example:** After dinner, clear the dishes and load the dishwasher.

> **Example:** Because the power went out last night, everyone was late for work this morning.

Use commas before *and, but, for, or, nor, so,* and *yet* when they join independent clauses.

> **Example:** Dan hit the ball, but Steve made the winning run.

Use commas to separate items in dates and addresses.

> **Example:** On January 14, 2007, I turned twelve.

> **Example:** Our new house is at 2314 Jackson Road, Fayetteville, GA 30214

Use a comma after the salutation of a friendly letter and after the closing of any letter.

> **Example:** Dear Eric,

> **Example:** Sincerely,

Use a comma after a name followed by an abbreviation such MD and DDS. Place another comma after the abbreviation if the sentence continues.

> **Example:** Robert Cook, DDS

> **Example:** Jack Martin, MD, has been our family doctor for years.

Use commas to set off parenthetical elements that interrupt the sentence.

> **Example:** Jordin Sparks, my favorite singer, performed last night.

> **Example:** The house, in my opinion, needs to be torn down.

Appositives and appositive phrases are usually set off by commas.

> **Example:** The documentary was about mobsters, people who participate in organized crime.

> **Example:** Stonewall Jackson, a Confederate general, was accidently shot by his own soldiers during the Civil War.

Words used in direct address are set off by commas.

> **Example:** Mr. Dale, your daughter is on the phone.

> **Example:** We want to thank you, Mrs. Jacobs, for your years of service.

> **Example:** Karen, take the dog for a walk.

Practice 1:   Commas
6C1d, 6W2d, 6W4c

Decide where the commas should be placed.

1.   The painting that one you liked was painted by Edouard Manet.

    A. after *painting* and before *was*   C. after *painting* and before *liked*

    B. after *painted*   D. after *liked*

2.   In the back of the closet Mara found her old teddy bear.

    A. after *back*   B. after *closet*   C. before *teddy*   D. before *found*

3.   Why was a letter dated June 5 2006 delivered so late?

    A. after *5* after *2006*   C. after *why* and after *letter*

    B. after *letter* and after *2006*   D. after *2006*

4. I met our neighbors Helen Barnet and Jarod Parks for lunch on Thursday.
   A. after *neighbors* and after *Parks*
   B. after *Barnet* and after *Parks*
   C. after *Parks* and after *lunch*
   D. after *lunch*

5. I need the address for Francis Aho MD.
   A. after *Francis*
   B. after *MD*
   C. after *Aho*
   D. No comma is needed.

6. Toni Morrison my favorite author is signing books at the local bookstore today.
   A. after *Morrison* and after *author*
   B. after *Morrison*
   C. after *books*
   D. after *books* and after *bookstore*

7. Did you hear that Aunt Marya a professional photographer bought a new car this year?
   A. after *Aunt* and after *Marya*
   B. after *Aunt* and after *photographer*
   C. after *Marya* and after *photographer*
   D. after *Marya*

8. I understand Andy that you want to study forensics.
   A. after *Andy*
   B. after *understand*
   C. after *understand* and after *Andy*
   D. after *Andy* and after *want*

SEMICOLONS

Use semicolons between items in a series if the items contain commas.

> **Example:** I have lived in Atlanta, Georgia; Springfield, Missouri; and Lakeland, Florida.

SEMICOLONS AND COMMAS IN SENTENCES

Use a semicolon between independent clauses if they are not joined by *for, and, nor, but, or, yet,* or *so.*

> **Example:** Our teacher leads a double life; she also runs a catering business.

> **Example:** Although bungee jumping is dangerous, we tried it; it was a huge adrenaline rush.

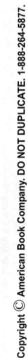

Use a semicolon between independent clauses joined by a conjunctive adverb or transitional expression. (a chart of conjunctive adverbs and transitional expressions would be good here)

> **Example:** I have pets; therefore, I often have animal hair on my clothes.

> **Example:** Chopping wood is no fun; on the other hand, a fire in the winter is always nice.

A semicolon may be needed to separate independent clauses that contain commas.

> **Example:** For band camp, you must bring an instrument, comfortable shoes, and your music; but extra food, medicine, and shower shoes are good items to bring that aren't on the list.

Practice 2: Semicolons
6C1d, 6W2d, 6W4c

Decide where the semicolon should be placed in each sentence.

1. I expected my furniture delivery in the morning however, I was still waiting at midnight.
   A. after *however*   B. after *morning*   C. after *delivery*   D. after *furniture*

2. The barn fell during the storm no animals were lost in the chaos.
   A. after *fell*   B. after *no*   C. after *storm*   D. after *animals*

3. A state's flag can contain a variety of symbols Georgia, for example, has the state seal surrounded by thirteen stars.
   A. after *Georgia*   B. after *symbols*   C. after *something*   D. after *example*

4. Jimmy Carter is from Plains, Georgia he served as the president from 1977 to 1981.
   A. after *Plains*   B. after *Georgia*   C. after *1971*   D. after *president*

5. The live oak is the official tree of Georgia the official song is "Georgia on My Mind."
   A. after *tree*

   B. after *song*

   C. after *the*

   D. after *Georgia*

COLONS

Use a colon before a list of items especially after expressions like *the following* and *as follows*.

> **Example:** This test will contain the following: multiple choice, true/false, short answer, and short essay response.

> **Example:** Please bring the following items to class on Tuesday: pencil, blue ink pen, three sheets of paper, folder with pockets, rubber bands, and a ruler.

Note: Do not put a colon after a verb or preposition.

WRONG – Pay special attention to: mosquitoes, fire ants, and spiders.

WRONG – You must bring: a pillow, sleeping bag, flashlight, and pocket knife.

Use a colon before a formal statement or a long quotation.

> **Example:** This is how I feel about dealing with people: "Do unto others as you would have them do unto you."

Note: Some quotations will need to be introduced by a comma. This depends on how you word the sentence. The previous sentence would need a comma if written as follows:

> **Example:** I agree with anyone who says, "Do unto others as you would have them do unto you."

Use a colon when writing out a time; place it between the hour and the minute.

> **Example:** The show starts at 7:45 p.m.

Use a colon between the chapter and the verse when referring to passages from Scripture.

> **Example:** Genesis 3:10

> **Example:** Qur'an 4:13

Use a colon after the salutation of a business letter.

> **Example:** Dear Human Resources Manager:

> **Example:** Dear Dr. Davis:

Practice 3:   Colons
6C1f, 6W2d, 6W4c

Proofread the following business letter. Add, delete, or replace punctuation if necessary.

Dear <u>Dr. Ingle,</u>
       1

    I am writing to confirm your speaking engagement at our university on <u>Friday April 15</u>. Dr. Manson will open
                          2

the session at <u>4:00 p.m</u>. with a brief introduction.
                 3

    We have the following audiovisual equipment available for your <u>use,</u> a slide projector, a DVD player, an
       4

overhead projector, and a CD player. Our computers are all Macs. Please let me know if you require any other equipment or supplies.

<u>Sincerely:</u>
    5

Dr. Janice Pataki

For each numbered item above, choose the best revision.

1.   Dear Dr. Ingle,
    A. Dear Dr Ingle,   C. Dear Dr. Ingle:
    B. Dear Dr. Ingle;   D. No change needed

2.   Friday April 15.
    A. Friday: April 15.   C. Friday; April 15.
    B. Friday, April 15.   D. No change needed

3.   4:00 p. m.
    A. 4.00 p.m.   C. 4,00 p.m.
    B. 4;00 p.m.   D. No change needed

4.   use, a slide
    A. use- a slide   C. use: a slide
    B. use; a slide   D. No change needed

5. Sincerely:
    A. Sincerely,
    B. Sincerely;

C. Sincerely'

D. No change needed

QUOTATION MARKS

Use quotation marks to enclose direct quotations—a person's exact words.

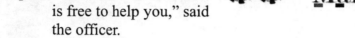

> **Example:** "Stand here until a clerk is free to help you," said the officer.

A direct quotation begins with a capital letter.

> **Example:** Tyler said, "The rain destroyed all the evidence for the case."

A direct quotation is set off from the rest of the sentence by a comma, a question mark, or an exclamation point (but not a period).

> **Example:** "They'll call a time out to drag the game on longer," said Jake.

> **Example:** "It doesn't matter because we won!" shouted Tim.

A period or a comma should always be placed inside the closing quotation marks.

> **Example:** Kim said, "That's a beautiful painting."

> **Example:** "My mother painted it," said Martha.

A question mark or an exclamation point should be placed inside the closing quotation marks when the quotation itself is a question or an exclamation. Otherwise, it should be placed outside.

> **Example:** "Who has a dollar I can borrow?" I asked.

> **Example:** Why did he say, "Time is always fleeting"?

When a quotation consists of several sentences, put quotation marks only at the beginning and end of the whole quotation.

> **Example:** "Today we will be reviewing how to dissect a worm. This experiment can be difficult for some, so I need everyone to be aware, and let me know if you think you're about to pass out."

When writing dialogue (conversation), begin a new paragraph every time the speaker changes.

> **Example:**
>
> Cynthia slowly reached for her coat and said, "I hope it doesn't get hot suddenly. I hate having to carry a coat around all day."

"The weatherman forecasted temperature in the thirties for the whole day, so I think you're safe to take it," replied Jean.

"Yeah, we all know how reliable the weatherman is, right?" retorted Cynthia.

Use single quotation marks to enclose a quotation within a quotation and to punctuate the title of a short work used within a quotation.

> **Example:** "Have you ever read 'The Eagle' by Tennyson?" asked Juan.

> **Example:** "My favorite lines are 'He watches from his mountain walls, and like a thunderbolt he falls'," replied Marion.

Practice 4: Quotation Marks
6C1f, 6W2d, 6W4c

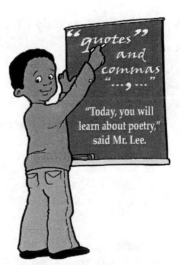

1. Which sentence is correctly using quotation marks?

   A. "Today you will be learning about poetry.

   B. 'Today you will be learning about poetry.'

   C. Today you will be learning about poetry"

   D. "Today you will be learning about poetry."

2. Which sentence is correctly using quotation marks and commas?

   A. "You will learn about poetic form as well as practice some writing in class, said Mrs. Williams.

   B. "You will learn about poetic forms as well as practice some writing in class, said Mrs. Williams."

   C. "You will learn about poetic forms as well as practice some writing in class," said Mrs. Williams.

   D. "You will learn about poetic forms as well as practice some writing in class", said Mrs. Williams.

3. Which sentence is correctly using quotation marks and commas?

   A. "I hate poetry because it never makes sense and is always about love," said Ahmed.

   B. 'I hate poetry because it never makes sense and is always about love," said Ahmed.

   C. "I hate poetry because it never makes sense and is always about love", said Ahmed.

   D. "I hate poetry because it never makes sense and is always about love, said Ahmed.

4. Which sentence is correctly using quotation marks and commas?

    A. "My favorite poem is O Captain! My Captain! by Walt Whitman.

    B. "My favorite poem is O Captain! My Captain! by Walt Whitman."

    C. "My favorite poem is "O Captain! My Captain!" by Walt Whitman."

    D. "My favorite poem is 'O Captain! My Captain!' by Walt Whitman."

5. Which sentence is correctly using quotation marks and commas?

    A. "I especially like the line, The ship has weather'd every rack, the prize we sought is won," said Catherine.

    B. "I especially like the line, "The ship has weather'd every rack, the prize we sought is won," said Catherine.

    C. "I especially like the line, 'The ship has weather'd every rack, the prize we sought is won'," said Catherine.

    D. "I especially like the line, 'The ship has weather'd every rack, the prize we sought is won,'" said Catherine.

APOSTROPHES

To form the possessive case of a singular noun, add an apostrophe and an *s*.

> **Example:** Milla's phone

> **Examples:** the teacher's pen
> the dog's bone

To form the possessive case of a plural noun ending in *s*, add only the apostrophe.

> **Example:** the Jacksons' house

> **Example:** the students' work
> the pets' food

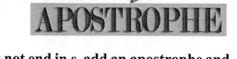

To form the possessive case of a plural noun that does not end in *s*, add an apostrophe and an *s*.

> **Example:** the children's toys
> the women's shoes   the mice's tails

Do not use an apostrophe with possessive personal pronouns.

> **Example:** Is the purse hers?

> **Example:** That is its nest.

Use an apostrophe to show where letters, numbers, or words have been left out in a contraction.

> **Example:** I will = I'll

> **Example:** where is = where's

> **Example:** 1995 = '95

> **Example:** of the clock = o'clock

Note: Be careful not to confuse possessive nouns with contractions

> **Example:** **It's** early. (It is early.) **Its** voice was creepy.

> **Example:** **You're** late. (You are late.) **Your** pizza was so flavorful!

Use an apostrophe and an *s* to form the plurals of letters, of numerals, and of words referred to as words.

> **Example:** Dot your *i*'s and cross your *t*'s.

> **Example:** Try not to begin sentences with so many *I*'s.

Practice 5: Apostrophes
6C1f, 6W2d, 6W4c

Pick the selection that correctly represents the possessive and/or plural relationship.

1. **desks of the engineers**
   A. the desk's engineers
   B. the desks' engineers
   C. the engineer's desks
   D. the engineers' desks

2. **chair of the speaker**
   A. the chair's speaker
   B. the chairs' speaker
   C. the speaker's chair
   D. the speakers' chair

3. **popcorn of the couple**
   A. the couple's popcorn
   B. the couples' popcorn
   C. the popcorns' couple
   D. the popcorn's couple

4. **color of the house**
   A. the house's color
   B. the houses' color
   C. the color's house
   D. the colors' house

5. **toys of the children**

    A. the childrens' toys

    B. the children's toys

    C. the toys' children

    D. the toy's children

6. **tunnels of the mines**

    A. the tunnels' mines

    B. the tunnel's mines

    C. the mines' tunnels

    D. the mine's tunnels

7. **faces of everyone**

    A. the faces' of everyone

    B. the face's of everyone

    C. everyones' faces

    D. everyone's faces

8. **jobs of the men**

    A. mens' jobs   B. men's jobs   C. Jobs' men   D. job's men

CHAPTER 2 SUMMARY

Commas go **between items in a series** and **adjectives in a row**.

Commas **set off items** such as introductory words and phrases, nonessential clauses and phrases, appositives, parenthetical elements, salutation and closings, abbreviations, and words of direct address.

Commas separate items in **dates and addresses**.

Commas **separate independent clauses** that have a coordinating conjunction.

Semicolons **separate items in a series** that already contains commas.

Semicolons **separate independent clauses** closely related and independent clauses joined by a conjunctive adjective or transitional expression.

Colons **introduce lists**, **long quotations,** and **business letter salutations**.

Colons **separate time** (hour:minute) and **scriptural references** (chapter:verse).

Quotation marks set off **direct quotations**.

Apostrophes **form the possessive** case of words.

Apostrophes **form contractions**.

CHAPTER 2 REVIEW

6C1d,f, 6W2d, 6W4c

Part I: Read the business letter below. Then answer the questions that follow.

5500 Ammons Road

Monroe, GA 30655

October 30, 2008

Dr. Toniesha Pollack

425 Lanyard Lane

Atlanta GA 30047

dear Dr. Pollack

I understand that you are seeking volunteers for the CommunityService projects which take place every weekend between 8 00 a.m. and 12 00 p.m. Our class advisor Mrs. Rico explained your program and suggested we volunteer to fulfill our service hours.

Many students have become interested in your program and wish to volunteer consequently I believe that we can fully staff one weekend a month from September to May. If you have any months where volunteers are especially low, please let us know. At first, your September volunteers will include the following students Thao Le Bryan Perez Catherine Blankenship Wayne Isaacs Dennis Batiste Duyen Vo Bryce Longmire and me

We have read all the literature that you provided and know what to expect Mrs. Rico explained that volunteers often dont assist in transporting and storing materials. Everyone is willing to help you out in any way that you need We are very excited to begin working and look forward to meeting you; Per your instruction we will arrive at 7 30 the first day for a short orientation

Sincerely

Fay Davis

Fay Davis

1   **What correction should be made in the business address?**

   A   comma after *Pollack*

   B   comma after *Atlanta*

   C   comma after *Georgia*

   D   no changes needed

2   **What correction should be made in the salutation?**

   A   Dear Dr. Pollack,

   B   Dear Dr. Pollack;

   C   Dear Dr. Pollack:

   D   no changes needed

3   **What correction should be made in the first body paragraph?**

   A   between 8:00 a.m. and 2:00 p.m.

   B   between 8:00 a.m. and 12:00 p.m.

   C   between 8'00 a.m. and 12'00 p.m.

   D   no changes needed

4   **What correction should be made in the second body paragraph?**

   A   wish to volunteer; consequently I believe

   B   wish to volunteer: consequently, I believe

   C   wish to volunteer; consequently, I believe

   D   no changes needed

5   **What correction should be made in the second body paragraph?**

   A   will include the following students: Thao Le, Bryan Perez, Catherine Blankenship, Wayne Isaacs, Dennis Batiste, Duyen Vo, Bryce Longmire, and me.

   B   will include the following students; Thao Le, Bryan Perez, Catherine Blankenship, Wayne Isaacs, Dennis Batiste, Duyen Vo, Bryce Longmire, and me.

   C   will include the following students. Thao Le; Bryan Perez; Catherine Blankenship; Wayne Isaacs; Dennis Batiste; Duyen Vo; Bryce Longmire; and me.

   D   no changes needed

6 **What correction should be made in the second body paragraph?**

   A We have read all the literature that you provided and know what to expect: Mrs. Rico explained that volunteers often dont assist in transporting and storing materials.

   B We have read all the literature that you provided and know what to expect; Mrs. Rico explained that volunteers often don't assist in transporting and storing materials.

   C We have read all the literature that you provided and know what to expect, Mrs. Rico explained that volunteers often don't assist in transporting and storing materials

   D no changes needed

7 **What corrections should be made in the second paragraph?**

   A Per your instructions we will arrive at 7:30 the first day for a short orientation.

   B Per your instruction, we will arrive at 7:30 the first day for a short orientation.

   C Per your instruction, we will arrive at 7;30 the first day for a short orientation?

   D no changes needed

8 **What corrections should be made in the closing?**

   A Sincerely:

   B Sincerely;

   C Sincerely,

   D no changes needed

Part II: For each numbered item, choose the letter of the best revision.

     What would you think if I told you <u>that I have webbed toes?</u> Would you find that bizarre
                                         1

and mind-blowing? It is actually much more common than you think. Webbed toes and fingers

are called syndactyly. It is a result of genetics <u>in some cases however most often</u> it is a result
                                                2

of a very <u>common action: smoking</u>. One in nine <u>expectant mothers' increases</u> the chances of
            3   4

syndactyly when she smokes according to information from the March of Dimes. Researchers

from the University of Pennsylvania reviewed medical records from 2001 to 2002. <u>According</u>
                                                             5

to USA Today on August 8 2007, "The researchers found that the more a woman smoked, the

6   7

greater the likelihood of finger or toe anomalies. It all points to one thing; don't smoke while

8

pregnant!

1 that I have webbed toes?

 A That I have webbed toes!

 B That I have webbed toes.

 C That I have webbed toes,

 D no change needed

2 in some cases however most often

 A in some cases, however, most often

 B in some cases: however, most often

 C in some cases; however, most often

 D no change needed

3 common action: smoking

 A common action, and smoking

 B common action. smoking

 C common action; smoking

 D no change needed

4 expectant mothers' increases

 A expectant mothers increases

 B expectant mothers's increase

 C expectant mother increases

 D no change needed.

5 According to USA Today

 A According to *USA Today*

 B According to "USA Today"

 C According to 'USA Today'

 D no change needed

6 <u>**August 8 2007,**</u>

    A   August 8. 2007,

    B   August 8: 2007,

    C   August 8, 2007,

    D   no change needed

7   **"The researchers found that the more a woman smoked, the greater the likelihood of finger or toe anomalies."**

    A   The researchers found that the more a woman smoked, the greater the likelihood of finger or toe anomalies."

    B   "The researchers found that the more a woman smoked, the greater the likelihood of finger or toe anomalies."

    C   'The researchers found that the more a woman smoked, the greater the likelihood of finger or toe anomalies."

    D   no changes needed

8   <u>**points to one thing; don't smoke**</u>

    A   points to one thing, don't smoke

    B   points to one thing "don't smoke"

    C   points to one thing-don't smoke

    D   no change needed

Chapter 3
Working with Verbs

This chapter addresses the following GPS-based CRCT standard:

ELA6C1	The student demonstrates understanding and control of the rules of the English language, realizing that usage involves the appropriate application of conventions and grammar in both written and spoken formats. The student
	a. Identifies and uses the eight basic parts of speech and demonstrates that words can be different parts of speech within a sentence.
	iv. Identifies and uses verbs – action (transitive/intransitive), linking, and state-of-being.
	v. Identifies and uses verb phrases – main verbs and helping verbs.

Verbs are necessary. In fact, without verbs, sentences could not exist. We need verbs in order to know what the subject of a sentence is like or what the subject does. In this chapter, we will look at different types of verbs and how they are used.

VERBS

A **verb** is a word that expresses action or state-of-being.

> **Example:** In 1961, Russia *launched* Yuri Gagarin into space. (action)

> **Example:** He *was* the first cosmonaut in the world. (state-of-being)

VERB TYPES

There are three types of verbs: *action*, *linking*, and *helping*.

An **action** verb expresses physical or mental action.

> **Example:** Hannah *works* for an amusement part. (physical)

> **Example:** Hannah *loves* her job. (mental)

A **transitive** verb is an action verb that requires an object (or objects) to complete its meaning.

> **Example:** Shannon Hale *published* her first **book** in 2003.

> > (**book** = direct object)

> **Example:** Justin *gave* his <u>sister</u> ***The Goose Girl*** for her birthday.

> > (<u>sister</u> = indirect object; ***The Goose Girl*** = direct object)

An **intransitive** verb is an action verb that does NOT require an object (or objects) to complete its meaning.

> **Example:** Ian *slept* for twelve hours last night! (no object)

Practice 1: Transitive and Intransitive Verbs
6C1a.iv

1. Which sentence uses a transitive verb?

    A. Nicole writes often for the school newspaper.

    B. Nicole writes a column for the school newspaper.

2. Which sentence uses an intransitive verb?

    A. Brandon sang four songs for the musical.

    B. Brandon sang with passion and fervor.

3. Which word in the sentence is the transitive verb?

    > When Jessica transferred to Brantley County Middle School, she only had a few friends.

    A. when   B. transferred   C. only   D. had

4. Which word in the sentence is the intransitive verb?

    > James mailed a letter to me yesterday, and it arrived today.

    A. mailed   B. yesterday   C. arrived   D. today

LINKING VERBS

A **linking verb** is a word that connects the subject to a **predicate noun** (which tells what the subject is) or a **predicate adjective** (which tells something about the subject). These complements are covered in more detail in chapter 7.

> **Example:** The youngest <u>player</u> in the NFL *is* **Amobi Okoye**.

> > (**Amobi Okoye** = predicate noun renaming <u>player</u>)

Example: The London District Catholic School Board's <u>record</u> of 15,851 simultaneous snow angels *is* **unbeaten**.

(**unbeaten** = predicate adjective describing <u>record</u>)

Some verbs related to the five senses (*look, sound, smell, feel,* and *taste*) can function as either action or linking verbs.

Example: Grandma's homemade apple pie *smelled* **wonderful**.

(*smelled* = linking verb, **wonderful** = predicate adjective)

Example: Madison *smelled* her grandma's homemade apple **pie** in the kitchen.

(*smelled* = action verb, **pie** = direct object)

Here is a list of some common linking verbs:

Linking Verbs				
am	became	feel	remain	taste
appear	become	grow	seem	was
are	been	is	smell	were
be	being	look	sound	will be

Practice 2: Linking Verbs
6C1a.iv

1. Which sentence uses a linking verb?

   A. The Georgian farmer grows soybeans.

   B. Soybeans grow well as a cover crop.

2. Which sentence uses a linking verb?

   A. Alexis felt horrible about talking back to her mother.

   B. After eating too much ice cream, Alexis felt a pain in her stomach.

3. Which word in the sentence is the linking verb?

> Even after losing the game, John seemed satisfied with his performance.

A. losing   B. seemed   C. satisfied   D. performance

4. Which word in the sentence is the linking verb?

> Five years ago, Emily moved from Atlanta to New York, but she is still a Braves fan.

A. ago   B. moved   C. to   D. is

5. Which word in the sentence is the linking verb?

> The gold necklace that Nicholas bought from the street vendor turned green.

A. bought   B. from   C. vendor   D. turned

6. Which word in the sentence is the linking verb?

> After years of practicing the violin, Stephanie finally became first chair.

A. after

B. practicing

C. finally

D. became

VERB PHRASES

A **helping verb** is a word (or words) added directly before a main verb (action or linking) to make a **verb phrase**. A verb phrase may be interrupted by other words.

> **Example:** Megan *has read* thirteen books this year.
>
> (*has* = helping verb; *read* = main action verb; *has read* = verb phrase)
>
> **Example:** With less time, she *would* not likely *have read* as many.
>
> (*would* and *have* = helping verbs; *read* = main action verb; *would have read* = verb phrase)
>
> **Example:** Megan *has been* an avid reader for years.
>
> (*has* = helping verb; *been* = main linking verb)

Here is a list of some common helping verbs:

Helping Verbs					
am	being	do	have	must	were
are	can	does	is	shall	will
be	could	had	may	should	would
been	did	has	might	was	

Practice 3: Verb Phrases
6C1a.v

1. In the sentence below, which is the main verb?

> Everyone had eaten by eight o'clock.

   A. everyone   B. had   C. eaten   D. before

2. In the sentence below, which is the helping verb?

> Austin has never seen the beach before.

   A. has   B. never   C. seen   D. before

3. In the sentence below, which is the verb phrase?

> By two o'clock, he will have swum for four straight hours.

   A. swum
   B. will swum
   C. have swum
   D. will have swum

4. In the sentence below, which is the verb phrase?

> Samantha was almost mistaken for her older sister.

A. mistaken

B. was mistaken

C. almost mistaken

D. was almost mistaken

VERB FORMS

Most verb endings follow simple patterns. Regular verbs take four possible **forms**: *present, past, present participle,* and *past participle.*

Verb Forms				
Verb	**Present**	**Past**	**Present Participle**	**Past Participle**
to walk	I **walk**.	I **walked**.	I am **walking**.	I have **walked**.
to study	I **study**.	I **studied**.	I am **studying**.	I have **studied**.

As you will see below, helping verbs may be added to these verb forms to indicate the tense (or time) of a particular action. There are six verb tenses:

Present Tense: something is happening now or habitual action.

> **Example:** David *plays* electric guitar.

Past Tense: something happened in the past but is not still happening.

> **Example:** David *played* electric guitar at a concert last night.

Future Tense: something will happen in the future.

> **Example:** David *will play* electric guitar on tour this summer.

Present Perfect Tense: something happened at one point in the past and continued up to the present.

> **Example:** David *has played* electric guitar for three years.

Past Perfect Tense: something happened before something else in the past.

> **Example:** David *had played* electric guitar for a year when he started taking lessons.

Future Perfect Tense: something will be completed at some point in the future.

> **Example:** Next year, David *will have played* the guitar for four years.

Verb Tenses		
Tense	**Simple**	**Perfect**
Past	David played.	David had played.
Present	David plays.	David has played.
Future	David will play.	David will have played.

Like nouns and pronouns (chapter 4), verbs can be singular or plural. Verbs must agree in number with their subjects (chapter 7). Singular subjects take singular verbs, and plural subjects take plural verbs. As a general rule, singular verbs end in an *s*; plural verbs do not. Irregular verb forms do not follow a set pattern.

Example: Taylor (singular subject) *eats* (singular verb) ice cream.

BUT

Rabbits (plural subject) *eat* (plural verb) carrots.

On the following pages are two lists of some common forms of verbs. The first list contains **regular verbs**. The second list contains **irregular verbs**. Review these lists, and learn the verb forms you do not know.

REGULAR VERB FORMS

Verb	Singular Form	Plural Form	Past Tense	Present Participle	Past Participle
ask	asks	ask	asked	asking	asked
call	calls	call	called	calling	called
fry	fries	fry	fried	frying	fried
pass	passes	pass	passed	passing	passed
receive	receives	receive	received	receiving	received
seem	seems	seem	seemed	seeming	seemed
wash	washes	wash	washed	washing	washed

IRREGULAR VERB FORMS

Verb	3rd Person Singular Form	Plural Form	Past Tense	Present Participle	Past Participle
be	is	are	was / were	being	been
burst	bursts	burst	burst	bursting	burst
choose	chooses	choose	chose	choosing	chosen
do	does	do	did	doing	done
draw	draws	draw	drew	drawing	drawn
eat	eats	eat	ate	eating	eaten
feel	feels	feel	felt	feeling	felt
fly	flies	fly	flew	flying	flown
give	gives	give	gave	giving	given
go	goes	go	went	going	gone
hear	hears	hear	heard	hearing	heard
know	knows	know	knew	knowing	known
leave	leaves	leave	left	leaving	left
make	makes	make	make	making	made
pay	pays	pay	paid	paying	paid
read	reads	read	read	reading	read
run	runs	run	ran	running	run
say	says	say	said	saying	said
see	sees	see	saw	seeing	seen
sing	sings	sing	sang	singing	sung
speak	speaks	speak	spoke	speaking	spoken
swim	swims	swim	swam	swimming	swum
take	takes	take	took	taking	taken
teach	teaches	teach	taught	teaching	taught
think	thinks	think	thought	thinking	thought
write	writes	write	wrote	writing	written

Note: The past participle of **freeze** is not **had freezed**. It is **had frozen**. The past tense of **sit** is not **sitted**. It is **sat**.

Practice 4: Verb Forms
6C1a

Choose the verb form that would BEST complete the sentence.

1. Courtney eventually _____ asleep after watching a long movie last night.
   A. falls   B. will fall   C. fell   D. has fallen

2. Ryan always _____ visiting his grandfather.
   A. enjoys   B. enjoy   C. have enjoyed   D. had enjoyed

3. I thought that I _____ someone calling my name.
   A. hear   B. hears   C. heard   D. had heard

4. Sometimes Kayla _____ off into space.
   A. stare
   B. stares
   C. had stared
   D. will have stared

5. Next summer, Christopher _____ for his uncle.
   A. work
   B. worked
   C. will work
   D. will have worked

6. Amanda _____ for an hour almost every night.
   A. jogs
   B. jogged
   C. have jogged
   D. will have jogged

7. Elizabeth _____ to a room full of people before.
   A. speaks   B. spoke   C. will speak   D. has spoken

8. Tyler _____ professionally for two years before he quit to pursue a career in acting.
   A. cook
   B. cooks
   C. will have cooked
   D. had cooked

9. When Melinda graduates from high school next month, she _____ school for twelve years.
   A. attends
   B. attended
   C. has attended
   D. will have attended

10. Tomorrow Lauren _____ her pen pal in Djibouti, Africa, a letter.
    A. write   B. wrote   C. has written   D. will write

CHAPTER 3 SUMMARY

A **verb** is a word that expresses action or state-of-being.

An **action** verb expresses physical or mental action.

A **transitive** verb is an action verb that requires an object to complete its meaning.

An **intransitive** verb is an action verb that does NOT require an object to complete its meaning.

A **linking verb** is a word that connects the subject to a **predicate noun** or a **predicate adjective**.

A **helping verb** is a word added directly before a main verb to make a **verb phrase.**

Regular verbs take four possible **forms**: *present, past, present participle,* and *past participle.*

There are six **verb tenses**: *present tense, past tense, future tense, present perfect tense,* and *past perfect tense,* and *future perfect tense.*

CHAPTER 3 REVIEW

6C1a.iv, a.v

1   Which sentence uses a transitive verb?

   A   Our school band will perform a concert this weekend.

   B   Our school band will also perform next month.

2   Which sentence uses an intransitive verb?

   A   Zachary studied for several hours last night.

   B   Zachary studied his notes and the chapter review.

3   Which word in the sentence is the transitive verb?

> When the tree fell, it made a terribly loud sound.

   A   fell

   B   made

   C   loud

   D   sound

4   Which word in the sentence is the intransitive verb?

> The crowd cheered ecstatically when she hit the game-winning home run.

   A   cheered

   B   hit

   C   game-winning

   D   run

5   Which sentence uses a linking verb?

   A   Rachel looked me in the eye when I walked by.

   B   Rachel looked disgusted with her test grade.

6   Which sentence uses a linking verb?

   A We were hiking in the woods last winter.

   B The dogwood trees were in full bloom last month.

7   Which word in the sentence is the linking verb?

> The game's outcome looked good until the other team's star player came to bat.

   A outcome

   B looked

   C came

   D bat

8   Which word in the sentence is the linking verb?

> Jacob became jealous when he realized what had happened.

   A became   **B** realized   **C** had   **D** happened

9   Which word in the sentence is the linking verb?

> They could smell the flowers in the air, and the sun felt warm on their faces.

   A could   **B** smell   **C** felt   **D** warm

10 Which word in the sentence is the linking verb?

> Joseph's shoes were dirty, and he tracked mud in the house all the way to his room.

   A were

   B dirty

   C tracked

   D to

11 In the sentence below, which is the main verb?

> I will never vote for him to be class president again.

A will   B never   C vote   D be

12 In the sentence below, which is the helping verb?

> If Ashley continues to train, she will be the winner one day.

A continues   B train   C will   D be

13 In the sentence below, which is the verb phrase?

> Alyssa has never achieved perfect attendance.

A has   C has achieved

B has never   D has never achieved

14 In the sentence below, which is the verb phrase?

> William has accomplished many of his personal goals this year.

A has   C has accomplished many

B has accomplished   D goals

For questions 15–24, choose the verb form that would BEST complete the sentence.

15 Emma ____ me every night at the same time.

A call

B calls

C had called

D will have called

16 On Monday I ____ Ethan if I could borrow one of his video games.

A ask   B asks   C asked   D had asked

17 Your balloon may have survived so far, but I think by the end of the week it ___.

A burst   B bursts   C has burst   D will burst

18 At the rate we are going, we _____ fifty cars by noon.

A wash

B washed

C have washed

D will have washed

19 He _____ in his test before he realized that he forgot to put his name on it.

A turn   B will turn   C has turned   D had turned

20 Grandma _____ chicken using the same recipe for twenty years.

A fries   B has fried   C have fried   D will fry

21 Every day, people _____ that things are going to get better.

A say   B says   C have said   D will have said

22 Alex _____ an English test during his first period class yesterday.

A takes   B took   C had taken   D has taken

23 From the age of five until today, Sophia _____ portraits of a range of people.

A draws

B drew

C has drawn

D will have drawn

24 In four years from now, my older brother _____ me how to drive.

A teaches

B taught

C will teach

D will have taught

Chapter 4
Nouns and Pronouns

This chapter addresses the following GPS-based CRCT standards:

ELA6C1	The student demonstrates understanding and control of the rules of the English language, realizing that usage involves the appropriate application of conventions and grammar in both written and spoken formats. The student
	a. Identifies and uses the eight basic parts of speech and demonstrates that words can be different parts of speech within a sentence.
	i. Identifies and uses nouns – abstract, common, collective, plural, and possessive.
	ii. Identifies and uses pronouns – personal, possessive, interrogative, demonstrative, reflexive, and indefinite.

What's in a Name

Early that day in class Matthew introduced himself, "Hi, how are you doing? My *noun* is Matt."

"Good to meet you, Matt. My *noun* is Mike." Michael replied. "I also go by the *nouns* student, son, and brother."

"That sounds familiar," Matthew noted with interest. "Sometimes people just call me *he* or *him*."

Michael agreed, "Oh, yeah, I know what *you* mean."

"How did you know people called me *you*?" Matthew asked surprisingly.

Taken just as much by surprise, Michael asked back, "And how did *you* know people called me *you*?"

This conversation may seem a bit confusing, but it's here to bring up a point: **nouns** and **pronouns** are names. Let's look a little closer.

NOUNS

A **noun** is the name of a person, place, thing, or idea.

> **Example:** Venus Williams, Puerto Rico, telephone, abundance

PROPER AND COMMON NOUNS

A **proper noun** is the name of a specific person, place, or thing. Proper nouns are always capitalized. A **common noun** is the name of any general person, place, thing, or idea. Common nouns are not capitalized unless they begin a sentence.

Proper Nouns	Common Nouns
Bill Cosby	comedian
Atlanta	city
Transformers™	toys

Practice 1: Proper and Common Nouns
6C1a.i

1. Which word in the sentence below is a proper noun?

> So many news reports focus on Iraq.

   A. so   B. many   C. on   D. Iraq

2. Which word in the sentence below is a common noun?

> Yesterday I walked to school with my sister.

   A. I   C. school

   B. walked   D. my

3. Which word in the sentence below is a common noun?

> Checkers is a highly underrated game, according to Marion Tinsley.

   A. checkers   C. according

   B. underrated   D. Marion Tinsley

4. Which word in the sentence below is a proper noun?

> Sports celebrities, like Tiger Woods, rarely escape the spotlight.

A. sports B. celebrities C. Tiger Woods D. spotlight

ABSTRACT AND COLLECTIVE NOUNS

An **abstract noun** is the name of an idea, characteristic, or quality. Abstract nouns are not capitalized unless they begin a sentence.

> **Example:** peace, warmth, success, honesty

A **collective noun** is the name of a group of people or things.

Collective Nouns			
army	collection	group	public
assembly	committee	herd	school
audience	company	jury	society
band	crew	navy	swam
board	crowd	number	team
chorus	family	orchestra	tribe
class	flock	pack	troop
club	government	panel	

Practice 2: Abstract and Collective Nouns
6C1a.l

1. Which word in the sentence below is an abstract noun?

> The students debated whether it took more courage to fight or run away.

A. students B. debated C. courage D. fight

2. Which word in the sentence below is a collective noun?

> A team of scientists agreed that Yangtze River dolphins are nearly extinct.

A. team

B. scientists

C. Yangtze River

D. dolphins

3. Which word in the sentence below is an abstract noun?

> The drama troupe exhibited excellence at its matinee performance.

A. drama   B. troupe   C. excellence   D. matinee

4. Which word in the sentence below is a collective noun?

> It gives me great joy to introduce our panel of judges.

A. it   B. joy   C. panel   D. judges

SINGULAR AND PLURAL NOUNS

A **singular noun** is the name of one person, place, thing, or idea. A **plural noun** is the name of more than one person, place, thing, or idea.

Earl of Sandwich

Person

Sandwich Islands

Place

Sandwich

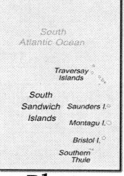

Thing

Singular Nouns	Plural Nouns
woman	women
region	regions
box	boxes
sheep	sheep

There are several rules associated with the making of **regular plural nouns**:

Rule 1. **Most nouns are made plural by adding the letter *s*.**

Examples: picture ⟶ pictures   tree ⟶ trees

Rule 2. **Nouns that end in *s, ch, sh, x,* or *z* are made plural by adding an *es*.**

Examples: church ⟶ churches   bush ⟶ bushes

Rule 3. **Nouns that end in a consonant and a *y*, are made plural by changing the *y* to an *i* and adding *es*. Nouns that end in a vowel and a *y* are made plural by adding an *s*.**

Examples: bunny ⟶ bunnies   story ⟶ stories
AND boy ⟶ boys   buoy ⟶ buoys

Rule 4. **Nouns that end in *f* or *fe* are usually made plural by changing the *f* to a *v* and adding *s* or *es*. There are some exceptions.**

Examples: knife ⟶ knives   wolf ⟶ wolves
BUT roof ⟶ roofs

Rule 5. **Some nouns maintain their Latin or Greek forms in the plural. In this case, nouns that end in *is* are made plural by replacing the *i* with an *e*. And sometimes, nouns that end with *us* are made plural by changing the *us* to an *i*.**

Examples: crisis ⟶ crises   thesis ⟶ theses
nucleus ⟶ nuclei   cactus ⟶ cacti

There are many exceptions to these five rules. If you are ever unsure of how to make a noun plural, look up the singular noun in a dictionary.

Here is a list of some **irregular plural nouns**.

Irregular Plurals				
potato	potatoes	**BUT**	cello	cellos
child	children	**AND**	woman	women
sheep	sheep	**AND**	deer	deer
scissors, pants, and glasses **ALWAYS** use a plural verb				

Practice 3:   Singular and Plural Nouns
6C1a.i

Which word BEST fills in the blank in the sentences below?

1. Shineka always signs her letters, "with hugs and ____."
   A. kisses   B. kiss

2. It's fun to go to the park and feed the ducks and the ____.
   A. gooses   B. geese

3. If you are traveling cross country in the snow, do you prefer snowshoes or ___.
   A. skies   B. skis

4. In Canada, I saw a grizzly bear, a fox, and several ____.
   A. moose   B. mooses

5. Rosa loves ____ in her garden salad.
   A. tomatos   B. tomatoes

6. At my Halloween party last year, there were three werewolves, two ____, and one Frankenstein in attendance.
   A. witchs   B. witches

7. Andre has three pet ____, but I have only one.
   A. snakes   B. snakess

8. My brother's room is so nasty that you could probably find a dozen different ____ growing there.
   A. fungi   B. funguses

POSSESSIVE NOUNS

A **possessive noun** shows ownership or attachment.

There are several **rules** associated with making nouns possessive:

Rule 1. **To make singular nouns possessive, add an apostrophe (') and an *s*.**

  Examples: Jose 's hobbies, the hamster's exercise wheel

Rule 2. **If the singular noun ends with an *s*, add an apostrophe and an *s*.**

  Examples: the bus's daily route, the cactus's thorns

Rule 3. **To make a plural noun ending in *s* possessive, add only the apostrophe.**

  Examples: the trees' shadows, the Joneses' residence

Rule 4. **If a plural noun does not end in *s*, the word is made possessive by adding an apostrophe and an *s*.**

  Examples: the men's restroom, the mice's food supply

Practice 4: Possessive Nouns
6C1a.i

Which word BEST fills in the blank in the sentences below?

1. Because of the value of ivory, ____ tusks were one in high demand.
   A. elephant's   B. elephants'

2. The ____ odor alerted Daniel to call the authorities.
   A. gas's   B. gas'

3. The ___ toys were left out in the rain.
   A. children's   B. childrens'

4. Her ___ tendency to break down was annoying.
   A. car's   B. cars's

5. That notebook is ____.
   A. Maria's

   B. Marias'

6. We all went to the ____ house for dinner last night.
   A. Smith's   B. Smiths'

PRONOUNS

A **pronoun** is a word that stands in the place of a noun. The word for which the pronoun stands is called its *antecedent*. The antecedent may be in the same sentence, in a previous sentence, or not given at all. People use pronouns so that they don't have to keep repeating the same noun.

> **Example:** The *girl* pitched a perfect game. *She* didn't let any hitter get to first base.

Girl is the antecedent of the pronoun *she*. *She* stands in for *girl*, so we don't have to repeat *girl*.

PERSONAL AND POSSESSIVE PRONOUNS

A **personal pronoun** refers to the speaker (first person), those being spoken to (second person), or those being spoken about (third person) in the sentence. Personal pronouns can be singular or plural.

> **Example:** **We** warned **you** about **them**.
>
> we = first person, plural
>
> you = second person, singular
>
> them= third person, plural

A personal pronoun that functions as a subject or predicate noun (see chapter 7) in a sentence is called a **nominative** pronoun.

> **Examples:** Callie and *I* don't know who called yesterday. (subject)
>
> It was *she* who called. (predicate noun)

A personal pronoun that functions as a direct object, indirect object (see chapter 7), or object of a preposition (see chapter 6) in a sentence is called an **objective** pronoun.

> **Examples:** Dante heard Jack and *him* in the hallway. (direct object)
>
> Louise gave *it* a chance. (indirect object)
>
> The music sounded good to both Jonathan and *him*. (object of a preposition)

A personal pronoun that shows ownership or attachment is a **possessive pronoun**.

> **Examples:** At the charity auction we sold *my* bike, *her* stamp collection, and *their* patio furniture. (all possessive pronouns)

The following table shows the relationship among first, second, and third person pronouns and nominative, objective, and possessive pronouns.

	Subjective	**Possessive**	**Objective**
Singular			
1st person	I	my, mine	me
2nd person	you	your, yours	you
3rd person	he	his	him
	she	her	her
	it	its	it
Plural			
1st person	we	our, ours	us
2nd person	you	your, yours	you
3rd person	they	their, theirs	them

Practice 5: Personal and Possessive Pronouns
6C1a.ii

1. Which word in the sentence below is a personal pronoun?

> Yesterday I spent the whole day at the mall.

A. yesterday   B. I   C. whole   D. the

2. The purse that Andrew found was ____.
   A. the   B. purse   C. Andrew   D. hers

Which word BEST fills in the blank in the sentences below?

3. The last song they played on the radio is ____ favorite.
   A. me   B. my

4. The coach gave ____ players a pep talk during half-time.
   A. we   B. us

5. Mom baked a cake for Rochelle and ____.
   A. me   B. I

6. After it started raining, Gwen and ____ wished they had not decided to walk home.
   A. her   B. she

INTERROGATIVE AND DEMONSTRATIVE PRONOUNS

An **interrogative pronoun** is used to begin a question. There are five interrogative pronouns: *what*, *which*, *who*, *whom*, and *whose*.

> **Examples:** *What* question is that? *Who* will help me? To *whom* should I address the letter? *Which* watch do you prefer?

Note: *Who* is nominative, and *whom* is objective.

> **Examples:** I want to know *who* ate the candy. (subject of the predicate *ate the candy*)

To *whom* should I give my extra candy? (object of the preposition *to*)

A **demonstrative pronoun** points out a particular person, place, thing, or idea. Some demonstrative pronouns are *this*, *that*, *these*, and *those*.

This is used to point out a singular object that is close by.

> **Example:** *This* is wonderfully detailed!

These is used to point out plural objects that are close by.

> **Example:** *These* are my new shoes.

That is used to point out a singular object far away.

> **Example:** *That* is my brother's jacket over there hanging on the chair.

Those is used to point out plural objects that are far away.

> **Example:** Can you pick *those* up and throw them in the recycling bin?

Note: *This*, *that*, *these*, and *those* can also be used as adjectives. They are demonstrative adjectives when they are followed by the noun they describe.

> **Examples:**
>> *This* jewelry is wonderfully detailed.
>> *These* Nikes™ are my new shoes.
>> *That* jacket is my brother's.
>> Can you pick up *those* pieces of paper and throw them in the recycling bin?

Practice 6: Interrogative and Demonstrative Pronouns
6C1a.ii

1. Which word from the sentence below is an interrogative pronoun?

   > Which of the contestants asked who the likely winner would be?

   A. which   B. who

2. Which word from the sentence below is an interrogative pronoun?

   > Whose favorite football team is the same as his?

   A. whose   B. his

3. Which word BEST fills in the blank in the sentence below?

   > _____ is going to be her lab partner?

   A. Who   B. Whom

4. Which word from the sentence below is a demonstrative pronoun?

   > This is the money that was missing.

   A. this   B. that

5. Which word from the sentence below is a demonstrative pronoun?

These cookies have fewer nuts than those.

A. these   B. those

INDEFINITE AND REFLEXIVE PRONOUNS

An **indefinite pronoun** stands for something that is unknown in meaning or quantity.

> **Examples:** *All* are encouraged to come to the pep rally. *Nobody* wants to miss the big game.

Here is a list of **indefinite pronouns:**

all	either	most	other(s)
another	everybody	much	several
any	everyone	neither	some
anybody	everything	no one	somebody
anyone	few	nobody	someone
anything	half	none	something
both	many	nothing	
each	more	one	

Like demonstrative pronouns, **indefinite pronouns** can also be used as indefinite adjectives when they are followed by the noun they describe.

> **Example:** *All* students are encouraged to come to the pep rally.

A **reflexive pronoun** indicates that the subject of the sentence also receives the action of the verb. Reflexive pronouns end in *self* or *selves*.

> **Examples:** Students who cheat are only hurting *themselves*.
>
> You gave *yourself* a haircut?
>
> She cheered up *herself* in spite of bad circumstances.

Practice 7:   Indefinite and Reflexive Pronouns
6C1a.ii

1. Which word from the sentence below is an indefinite pronoun?

Some students would give anything to be a famous actor.

A. some   B. anything

2. Which word from the sentence below is an indefinite pronoun?

> Neither of the horses has won more races than Sea Biscuit.

    A. neither

    B. more

3. Which word BEST fills in the blank in the sentence below?

> Daniell and Robin quizzed _____ the night before taking the test.

    A. herself

    B. themselves

4. Which word BEST fills in the blank in the sentence below?

> The baby bear learned to feed _____.

    A. itself

    B. themselves

CHAPTER 4 SUMMARY

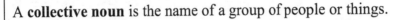

Nouns and **pronouns** are names.

A **proper noun** is the name of a specific person, place, or thing.

A **common noun** is the name of any general person, place, thing, or idea.

An **abstract noun** is the name of an idea, characteristic, or quality.

A **collective noun** is the name of a group of people or things.

A **singular noun** is the name of one person, place, thing, or idea.

A **plural noun** is the name of more than one person, place, thing, or idea.

A **possessive noun** shows ownership or attachment.

A **pronoun** is a word that stands in the place of a noun.

The word for which the pronoun stands is called its *antecedent*.

A **personal pronoun** refers to the speaker (first person), those being spoken to (second person), or those being spoken about (third person) in the sentence.

A personal pronoun that functions as a subject or predicate noun in a sentence is called a **nominative** pronoun.

A personal pronoun that functions as a direct object, indirect object, or object of a preposition in a sentence is called an **objective** pronoun.

A personal pronoun that shows ownership or attachment is a **possessive pronoun**.

An **interrogative pronoun** is used to begin a question.

A **demonstrative pronoun** points out a particular person, place, thing, or idea.

An **indefinite pronoun** stands for something that is unknown in meaning or quantity.

A **reflexive pronoun** indicates that the subject of the sentence also receives the action of the verb.

CHAPTER 4 REVIEW

6C1a.i,a.ii

1 Which word in the sentence below is a common noun?

Australia published its first comic book in 1931.

A Australia   B published   C comic   D book

2 Which word in the sentence below is a proper noun?

Comics published after 1945 are from the Atomic Age.

A comics

B published

C 1945

D Atomic Age

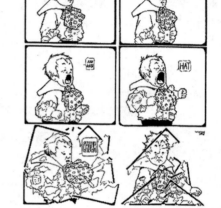

3 Which word in the sentence below is a proper noun?

Japanese comics began to look like they do today beginning after World War II.

A Japanese   C today

B they   D World War II

4 Which word in the sentence below is a abstract noun?

Photography is the process of producing images on a surface that is sensitive to light.

A process   B images   C surface   D sensitive

5 Which word in the sentence below is a collective noun?

A group of family members reserved a section of seats on the bus.

A group   B family   C members   D section

6   **Which word in the sentence below is a collective noun?**

> The magician skillfully shuffled the deck of cards in front of the audience.

A magician   **B** deck   **C** cards   **D** audience

7   **Which word BEST fills in the blank in the sentences below?**

> The first ____ of mangoes is no fresher than the second.

A crop   **B** crops

8   **Which word BEST fills in the blank in the sentences below?**

> To prepare for the lumberjack competition, she brought one saw and three ___.

A axs   **B** axes

9   **Which word BEST fills in the blank in the sentences below?**

> The huge middle school campus had three gymnasiums and two ____.

A libraries   **B** librarys

10   **Which word BEST fills in the blank in the sentences below?**

> The view was mesmerizing, full of mountain peaks and several low lying ___.

A vallies   **B** valleys

11   **Which word BEST fills in the blank in the sentences below?**

> The idea of a cat having nine ___ probably originated in Egypt.

A lives   **B** lifes

12 Which word BEST fills in the blank in the sentences below?

_____ family has instilled in him a strong work ethic.

A Charles's   **B** Charles

13 Which word BEST fills in the blank in the sentences below?

A _____ tail can be used like a hand.

A monkey's   **B** monkeys'

14 Which word BEST fills in the blank in the sentences below?

_____ reputation for high-style shopping began in the 1950s.

A Beverly Hills's   **B** Beverly Hills'

15 Which word BEST fills in the blank in the sentences below?

The _____ playground was recently updated.

A childrens'   **B** children's

16 Which word BEST fills in the blank in the sentences below?

Grandpa brought gifts for my sister and _____.

A me   **B** I

17 Which word BEST fills in the blank in the sentences below?

Billy and ___ won last year's ping pong doubles championship.

A him

B he

18 **Which word in the sentence below is a personal pronoun?**

> Jennifer and Anthony visited their relatives in Florida this summer.

A Anthony   **B** their   **C** in   **D** this

19 **Which word in the sentence below is a personal pronoun?**

> We were unaware of the need to study so hard.

A we   **B** the   **C** need   **D** so

20 **Which word in the sentence below is an interrogative pronoun?**

> Which of these test questions is the easiest?

A which   **B** of   **C** these   **D** the

21 **Which word in the sentence below is a demonstrative pronoun?**

> These questions may be easier than those.

A these   **B** may   **C** than   **D** those

22 **Which word in the sentence below is a demonstrative pronoun?**

> This is one of those questions that makes you think.

A this   **B** one   **C** those   **D** that

23 **Which word in the sentence below is an indefinite pronoun?**

> Anyone who studies well should find herself successful.

A anyone   **B** who   **C** well   **D** herself

24 Which word in the sentence below is an indefinite pronoun?

Each student did as well on the test as the other.

A each

B as

C the

D other

25 Which word in the sentence below is a reflexive pronoun?

They took pride in themselves and in their school.

A they

B themselves

C and

D their

Chapter 5
Adjective and Adverbs

English Language Arts

This chapter addresses the following GPS-based CRCT standards:

ELA6C1	The student demonstrates understanding and control of the rules of the English language, realizing that usage involves the appropriate application of conventions and grammar in both written and spoken formats. The student
	a. Identifies and uses the eight basic parts of speech and demonstrates that words can be different parts of speech within a sentence.
	iii. Identifies and uses adjectives—common, proper, and demonstrative.
	vi. Identifies and uses adverbs.

What if you wanted to tell your best friend about your first day of middle school, but you couldn't use any adjectives or adverbs? For example, you couldn't say that there was a *long* line of students in the cafeteria. You also couldn't explain that you had to travel *quickly* between classes to avoid being late. Your story would be very bland and uninteresting. In fact, without being able to use adjectives or adverbs, you might not be able to tell the story you really want to. This is why adjectives and adverbs, our descriptor and modifier words, are so important.

Adjectives are words used to modify nouns and pronouns. **Adverbs** are words used to modify verbs, adjectives, and other adverbs. Adjectives and adverbs make the difference between "a boy walking down the street" and "a *happy, young* boy skipping *excitedly* down a *city* block." They make both our writing and speaking come alive to listeners and readers. Let's begin with a look at adjectives.

ADJECTIVES

Generally, **adjectives** are words that modify nouns or pronouns. To modify means to describe. Adjectives also help to add information for the listener or the reader. Specifically, they tell us what kind, which one, how much, or how many. The most frequently used adjectives, *a, an,* and *the,* are called **articles**. Here are some examples of adjectives at work:

> Rita wears *red* shoes and *blue* jeans almost every day.

In this sentence, the words *red* and *blue* are adjectives. They modify the nouns *shoes* and *jeans,* telling us what kind of shoes and what kind of jeans Rita wears. Here is another example.

> The *last* student to turn in his paper, Ben felt confident that his grade would be an "A."

In this sentence, last is an adjective that modifies the noun student. It tells us which one.

> There are *forty-two* jellybeans in *the* jar.

In this sentence, forty-two is an adjective that modifies jellybeans. It tells us how many jelly beans are in the jar. The article *the* is also an adjective. It points out which jar.

Note: Possessive pronouns such as *his, her, its, our* and *their* can also be used as adjectives.

Practice 1:   Using Common Adjectives

6C1a.iii

Identify the adjective in each sentence.

1. Planning for the semester, Michelle stored twenty pencils in her pouch.

   A. pencil   C. stored

   B. twenty   D. all of the above

2. The agile dancer sailed across the floor.

   A. dancer   B. floor   C. sailed   D. agile

3. Her parents watched from the front row.

   A. her   B. parents   C. front   D. both A and B

4. The bored puppy began to chew his owner's favorite shoes.

   A. favorite

   B. bored

   C. shoes

   D. both A and B

5. The angry business man tossed financial papers from the window.
    A. angry
    B. business
    C. financial
    D. all of the above

6. I placed a book on the table, planning to read it after dinner.
    A. a
    B. table
    C. dinner
    D. all of the above

7. The nervous adolescent paced back and forth across the pink rug that covered the floor.
    A. the
    B. nervous
    C. pink
    D. all of the above

PROPER ADJECTIVES

Another type of adjective is the **proper adjective**. Proper adjectives are formed from proper nouns and begin with capital letters. Look at the following chart to note examples of how proper nouns become proper adjectives.

Proper Nouns	Proper Adjectives
America	American patriotism
Korea	Korean food
Georgia	Georgia student
Ernõ Rubik	Rubik's Cube

Let's look at some sentence examples.

We went to the food court in search of *Japanese* restaurants.

In this sentence, the word *Japanese* is a proper adjective that modifies restaurants. It is formed from the proper noun Japan.

In our language arts class, we are studying *Shakespearean* drama.

In this sentence, the word *Shakespearean* modifies drama. It is a proper adjective formed from the proper noun Shakespeare.

Practice 2:   Using Proper Adjectives
6C1a.iii

Identify the proper adjectives in the following sentences.

1. The language arts teacher used Stevie Wonder songs to demonstrate poetic devices.

    A. poetic

    B. language arts

    C. Stevie Wonder

    D. none of these

2. Greek art was the focus of our first unit.

    A. art

    B. Greek

    C. focus

    D. none of these

3. The Atlanta night life is full of unique music and good restaurants.

    A. Atlanta

    B. night life

    C. restaurants

    D. none of these

4. For breakfast, we often have Canadian bacon and eggs.

    A. eggs

    B. bacon

    C. Canadian

    D. none of these

5. My French tutor rarely speaks to me in English.

    A. French

    B. tutor

    C. English

    D. both A and C

DEMONSTRATIVE ADJECTIVES

Another adjective type, the **demonstrative adjective**, tells us specifically which one. Demonstrative adjectives are *this, that, these,* and *those*. We use *this* and *these* to refer to things that are closer to the speaker. *That* and *those* are used to refer to things that are not as close to a speaker. Just like other adjectives, demonstratives are used to modify nouns and pronouns in a sentence. Let's take a look at some demonstrative adjectives in sentences.

> *This* story is very long.
>
> I do not like *these* types of movies.
>
> *That* play will feature many of our sixth grade classmates.
>
> I will not stand for *those* sorts of insults from anyone.

Practice 3: Using Demonstrative Adjectives
6C1a.iii

In each of the following sentences, identify the nouns or pronouns being modified by demonstrative adjectives.

1. During this unit, we will discuss the rise and fall of ancient civilization.
   A. during   B. unit   C. discuss   D. civilization

2. We will have to use these dry erase markers instead of those.
   A. dry erase markers   C. instead
   B. we   D. none of these

3. That car was going too fast to come to a sudden stop.
   A. sudden   C. car
   B. that   D. stop

In 4-5, decide which words are used as demonstrative adjectives.

4. The low test scores mean that we will have to start over and review those skills.
   A. that   B. those   C. both A and B

5. That train would have to have been traveling very quickly in order to have hit these cars with such force.
   A. that   B. these   C. both A and B

ADVERBS

Adverbs, like adjectives, are also modifiers. Instead of modifying nouns and pronouns as adjectives do, adverbs modify verbs, adjectives, and other adverbs. Adverbs tell us when, where, how, or to what extent (how much or how long). Many adverbs end in the suffix –ly. However, not all adverbs have this characteristic, so be sure to consider how words are being used in the sentence. Let's take a look at some adverb examples.

When	I went to school *yesterday*. *Yesterday* modifies *went* and tells when.
	Marlee *often* goes camping. *Often* modifies *goes* and tells when.
Where	We will camp *here* and hike again in the morning. *Here* modifies *camp* and tells where.
	Open the box, and look *inside* to find the surprise. *Inside* modifies *look* and tells where.

How	We moved *quickly* to get out of the rain. *Quickly* modifies *moves* and tells how.
	Jessie *carefully* removed the eggs from the carton. *Carefully* modifies *removed* and tells how.
To What Extent	We *rarely* have pop quizzes in social studies. *Rarely* modifies *have* and tells to what extent.
	A traffic jam *almost* occurred in the busy sixth grade hallway. *Almost* modifies *occurred* and tells to what extent.

Practice 4: Using Adverbs
6C1a.vi

Read each sentence, and identify the adverb.

1. I ran quickly from my bus to the building.

    A. from   B. to   C. quickly   D. building

2. Let's split up and plan to meet here for lunch.

    A. split

    B. up

    C. meet

    D. here

3. We almost ran out of supplies during the rainy season.

    A. almost   B. ran   C. of   D. rainy

4. I never neglect my test study time.

    A. neglect   B. my   C. never   D. study

5. The crime took place suddenly, catching its victim off guard.

    A. catching   B. suddenly   C. the   D. off

CHAPTER 5 SUMMARY

Adjectives are words that modify nouns or pronouns.

Adjectives help to add information for the listener or the reader.

They tell us what kind, which one, how much, or how many.

The most frequently used adjectives, *a, an,* and *the,* are called articles.

Proper adjectives are formed from proper nouns and begin with capital letters.

Demonstrative adjectives tell us specifically which one.

Demonstrative adjectives are *this*, *that*, *these*, and *those*.

Adverbs modify verbs, adjectives, and other adverbs.

Many, but not all, adverbs end in the suffix –ly.

Adverbs tell us when, where, how, or to what extent (how much or how long).

CHAPTER 5 REVIEW

6C1a.iii,a.vi

For questions 1–5, identify the *adjective* in each sentence.

1   The frightening tornado caught many city residents off guard.

    A frightening

    B city

    C off

    D both A and B

2   These index cards will not be enough to complete the entire research process.

    A these

    B index

    C the

    D all of the above

3   Charlize is known for her fabulous fashion taste and stylish trend-setting clothes.

    A trend-setting

    B clothes

    C taste

    D all of the above

4   Please put my red shoes on the top shoe rack.

    A red

    B shoe

    C the

    D all of the above

5 I will not bring that lunch box every day, once I am
   in the sixth grade.

    A that

    B sixth

    C once

    D both A and B

For questions 6–10, identify the adverb in *each* sentence.

6 It is best that we move steadily to keep pace with the rest of the runners.

    A pace

    B is

    C steadily

    D none of these

7 At this rate, we will never finish washing these dishes.

    A at

    B never

    C these

    D finish

8 I will gladly attend morning help sessions for math if breakfast will be served.

    A morning

    B gladly

    C will

    D none of these

9 The bus leaves from the corner every day at noon.

    A every day

    B leaves

    C from

    D the

10 After school and extra-curricular activities, there is hardly any time to spend with my family.

   A after

   B extra

   C hardly

   D none of these

For questions 11–15, decide if the underlined word is being used as an adjective or an adverb.

11 There will <u>never</u> be a grandmother who is as special as mine.

   A adjective

   B adverb

12 My <u>everyday</u> shoes are dirty and worn.

   A adjective

   B adverb

13 We will meet here <u>every day</u> after school.

   A adjective

   B adverb

14 The <u>quick</u> girl was able to out sprint all competitors.

   A adjective

   B adverb

15 Moving <u>quickly</u>, the girl was able to out sprint all competitors.

   A adjective

   B adverb

Chapter 6
Prepositions, Conjuctions, Interjections

This chapter addresses the following GPS-based CRCT standard:

ELA6C1	The student demonstrates understanding and control of the rules of the English language, realizing that usage involves the appropriate application of conventions and grammar in both written and spoken formats. The student
	a. Identifies and uses the eight basic parts of speech and demonstrates that words can be different parts of speech within a sentence.
	vii. Identifies and uses prepositional phrases (preposition, object of the preposition, and any of its modifiers).
	viii. Identifies and uses conjunctions – coordinating, correlative, and common subordinating.
	ix. Identifies and uses interjections.

In the last three chapters, you learned about five of the eight parts of speech. This chapter will explain three more—**prepositions**, **conjunctions**, and **interjections**. You will learn about each part of speech in detail. This way, you can easily identify them and understand how each is used in a sentence.

PREPOSITIONS

A **preposition** is a word that relates nouns or pronouns to other words in a sentence. Prepositions show relationships in time or space. For example, words like *up*, *down*, *in*, and *out* show location.

> Basketball season **at** school begins **in** three weeks.
>
> We finally get to play **inside** the new gym.
>
> They built the gym **behind** the school and **beside** the field.

A **prepositional phrase** includes a preposition followed by a noun or pronoun that acts as the **object** of that preposition. There may also be modifiers (like adjectives) for the object . A prepositional phrase can function as a noun, an adjective, or an adverb. In these examples, the propositions are **bold,** and the objects are <u>underlined</u>.

> The little boy hid **behind** <u>the chair</u>, so he could scare his sister.
>
> Tony practices every day because he wants to be **in** <u>the marching band</u>.
>
> Jacob and Lori went **to** <u>the grocery store</u> yesterday and bought some ice cream.

When a **pronoun** is the object of the preposition, it must be in the objective case. Refer to chapter 4 for more practice with pronouns.

> Bill was very upset when the water balloon fell **on** <u>him</u>.
>
> Sheila and I were the only friends who really stood **by** <u>her</u>.
>
> It is a waste of time **for** <u>you and me</u> to drive all this way for the game.

Here is a list of common prepositions.

Prepositions				
aboard	away from	down	like	throughout
about	because of	during	near	till
above	before	except	of	to
according to	behind	for	off	together with
across	below	from	on	toward
after	beneath	in	onto	under
against	beside	in addition to	opposite	underneath
along	besides	in back of	out	until
alongside	between	in front of	outside of	unto
amid	beyond	in place of	over	up
among	by	in regard to	past	up to
apart from	by means of	in spite of	prior to	upon
around	concerning	inside	regarding	with
aside from	considering	instead of	since	within
at	despite	into	through	without

Practice 1: Prepositions
6C1a.vii

1. Which word in the sentence is a preposition?

> Susan taught her little sister how to tie her shoes when she was in kindergarten.

A. her

B. how

C. when

D. in

2. Which of the underlined words is a preposition?

> The <u>hunter</u> pulled the <u>alligator</u>, snapping furiously, <u>from</u> the <u>water</u>.

A. hunter   B. alligator   C. from   D. water

3. How many prepositions are in this sentence?

> Found on the islands of the Indonesian archipelago at the start of the twentieth century, Komodo dragons are endangered, with only a few thousand left.

A. two   B. three   C. four   D. five

4. Which word is the object of the underlined preposition?

> Julianne loves to visit her aunt <u>in</u> New York every summer.

A. Julianne   B. New York   C. visit   D. summer

5. Which of the underlined words is a preposition?

> Tony <u>Hawk</u> has <u>won</u> dozens <u>of</u> skateboard <u>competitions</u>.

A. Hawk

B. won

C. of

D. competitions

6. Which pronoun correctly fills in the blank?

> The naughty little boy stole the stuffed animal from _____ .

   A. her   B. I   C. they   D. she

7. Which word is the object of the underlined preposition?

> The Mariana Trench is the deepest spot <u>in</u> any ocean of the world.

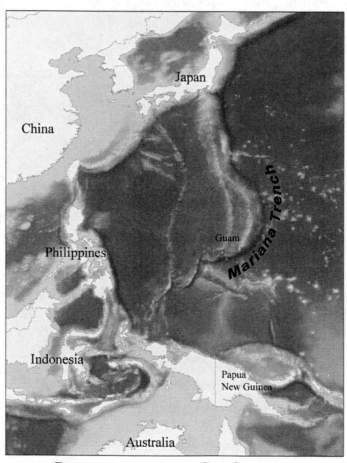

   A. any   B. ocean   C. of   D. world

8. Which word in this sentence is a preposition?

> I wish the ribbons were equally distributed among the teams.

   A. wish   B. were   C. among   D. teams

CONJUNCTIONS

A **conjunction** is a word that connects other words or groups of words. There are three types of conjunctions.

Coordinating conjunctions connect related words, phrases (groups of words), or clauses (groups of words with a subject and verb). Coordinating conjunctions connect things of equal importance. There is an easy way to remember the list of coordinating conjunctions—just remember FANBOYS! (*for, and, nor, but, or, yet, so*)!

Examples: <u>Sam</u> **and** <u>Marcus</u> tried out for the basketball team. (*And* connects two related words.)

A mail carrier does her job <u>in the rain</u>, <u>in the sleet</u>, **or** <u>in the snow</u>. (*Or* connects three prepositional phrases.)

<u>The team is very competitive</u>, **so** <u>they practice all the time</u>. (*So* connects two independent clauses.)

Correlative Conjunctions are pairs of conjunctions that work together to connect sentence parts.

Correlative Conjunctions
either…or
neither…nor
both…and
not only…but also
whether…or

When using correlative conjunctions, the words, phrases, or clauses that are linked must be the same type. For example, nouns must stay with nouns, adjectives with adjectives, clauses with clauses, and so on.

> **Examples:** This meal is **both** <u>delicious</u> **and** <u>nutritious</u>. (*Both...and* connects two adjectives.)
>
> Marcus loves playing sports **not only** <u>in the summertime</u>, **but also** <u>in the wintertime</u>. (*Not only...but also* connects two prepositional phrases.)

> **Example:** **Either** <u>he goes</u>, **or** <u>I go</u>. (*Either...or* connects two independent clauses.)

Subordinating conjunctions connect dependent clauses to independent clauses. A dependent clause cannot stand alone as a sentence. It must *depend* on an independent clause, which is a clause that can stand alone as a sentence and make sense. The subordinating conjunction may or may not appear directly between the clauses it joins.

> **Example:** <u>All players will have to pass a physical</u> **before** <u>they can play</u>.
>
> (independent clause)　　　　　　　(dependent clause)

> **Example:** **After** <u>the party was over</u>, <u>Melinda did not have a ride home</u>.
>
> (dependent clause)　　　　(independent clause)

Below is a box that gives examples of each type of conjunction.

Conjunctions					
Coordinating	**Correlative**	**Subordinating**			
and	both...and	after	before	rather than	until
but	either...or	although	if	since	when
for	if...then	as	if only	so that	whenever
nor	just as...so	as if	in order that	that	where
or	neither...nor	as long as	now that	though	whereas
so	not only...but also	as though	once	till	wherever
yet	whether...or	because	provided that	unless	while

Practice 2: Conjunctions
6C1a.viii

1. Which word in the sentence is a subordinating conjunction?

> Because the puppy enjoys chewing shoes, Suzanne often has to replace her slippers.

   A. Because   B. puppy   C. often   D. replace

2. Which word in the sentence is a coordinating conjunction?

> I am terrified of roller coasters, but I love going to Six Flags.

   A. am

   B. of

   C. but

   D. to

3. Which type of conjunction is the underlined group of words?

> Jason will choose to take <u>either</u> biology <u>or</u> Spanish in the spring.

   A.   C. correlative

   B. coordinating   D. subordinating

4. Which word in the sentence is a coordinating conjunction?

> Timothy loves to eat peanuts and popcorn when he goes to baseball games.

   A. loves   B. and   C. goes   D. to

5. Which type of conjunction is the underlined group of words?

> <u>If</u> you want to make a better grade, <u>then</u> you must study harder.

   A. not a conjunction   C. correlative

   B. coordinating   D. subordinating

6. Which type of conjunction is the underlined word?

> Jacqueline gets nervous <u>when</u> she performs in front of an audience.

A. not a conjunction

B. coordinating

C. correlative

D. subordinating

7. How many conjunctions are in this sentence?

> My mother told me I could invite three friends to the movies, so I chose Henry, Martin, and Jessica.

A. one   B. two   C. three   D. four

8. Which type of conjunction is the underlined word?

> Rico is my favorite person <u>in</u> the world.

A. not a conjunction

B. coordinating

C. correlative

D. subordinating

INTERJECTIONS

Interjections are words or phrases that express strong feeling or surprise. *Wow!*, *Oh no!*, and *Yikes!* are all interjections. Various emotions can be displayed by interjections. Interjections are usually followed by exclamation points. They also can be set off by commas when the emotion is not as strong.

Examples: **Oh!** I had no idea I was so late.

Well, I guess there's no use in complaining.

My goodness!

Practice 3: Interjections
6C1a.ix

1. Choose the BEST interjection for the feeling shown in parentheses.

> (Joy)! We won the championship game!

A. Oh no   B. Hooray   C. Well   D. Goodness

2. Which of the underlined words is an interjection?

> "<u>Lions</u> and tigers <u>and</u> bears, <u>oh my</u>!" Dorothy <u>exclaimed</u>.

A. Lions

B. and

C. oh my

D. exclaimed

3. Which emotion does the underlined interjection display?

> <u>Ouch</u>! That bee just stung me!

A. pity   B. pleasure   C. surprise   D. pain

4. Choose the appropriate interjection for the feeling shown in the parentheses.

> (Surprise)! I didn't expect to see you here!

A. Oh my gosh   B. Yahoo   C. Aw   D. Ouch

5. Which emotion does the underlined interjection display?

> <u>Uh</u>, I don't know the answer.

A. impatience   B. hesitation   C. joy   D. pain

6. Which of the underlined words is an interjection?

> <u>Wow</u>! <u>What</u> a <u>great</u> <u>present</u>!

A. Wow

B. What

C. great

D. present

7. Choose the appropriate interjection for the feeling shown in the parentheses.

    > (Disappointment), we missed the train.

    A. Yippee   B. Wow   C. Oh no   D. My goodness

8. Which emotion does the underlined interjection display?

    >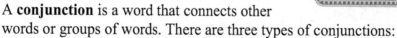
    > Well, I guess we could stop by the movie rental store on the way home.

    A. joy   B. hesitation   C. dismay   D. surprise

CHAPTER 6 SUMMARY

A **preposition** is a word that relates nouns or pronouns to other words in a sentence.

Prepositional phrases are phrases that include a preposition followed by a noun or pronoun acting as the **object** of the preposition.

When a **pronoun** is the **object** of the preposition, it must be in the objective case.

A **conjunction** is a word that connects other words or groups of words. There are three types of conjunctions:

-   **Coordinating conjunctions** connect related words, groups of words, or sentences of equal importance.
-   **Correlative conjunctions** are pairs of conjunctions that work together to connect sentence parts.
-   **Subordinating conjunctions** connect dependent clauses to independent clauses.

An **interjection** is a word or phrase that is used to express strong feeling or surprise.

Chapter 6 Review

6C1a.vii, a.viii, a.ix

1 How many prepositions are in this sentence?

> The Union Army occupied the city for three years during the Civil War.

A one   **B** two   **C** three   **D** four

2 Which emotion does the underlined interjection display?

> Wow! I can't believe you got to meet David Beckham!

A joy   **C** impatience

B pain   **D** disappointment

3 Which word in the sentence is a coordinating conjunction?

> I enjoy cereal for breakfast, but Derek likes oatmeal.

A enjoy   **B** for   **C** but   **D** likes

4 Which word is the object of the underlined preposition?

> Cats are important to many cultures because they are clean, independent, and hunt well.

A many   **B** cultures   **C** hunting   **D** skills

5 What type of conjunction is the underlined word?

> Since Mary enjoys Carrie Underwood so much, her boyfriend bought her tickets to Carrie's next concert.

A not a conjunction   **C** correlative

B coordinating   **D** subordinating

6 Choose the appropriate interjection for the emotion shown in the parentheses.

> (Pity), I'm sorry you got a poor grade on your report.

A Wow

B Aw

C Yay

D Hey

7 Which of the underlined words in the sentence is a preposition?

> My parents <u>and</u> I are taking a trip <u>to</u> <u>the</u> Grand Canyon <u>this</u> summer.

A and   **B** to   **C** the   **D** this

8 Which of the underlined words in this sentence is an interjection?

> "<u>Hey</u>! Come <u>back</u> here with my purse!" the <u>surprised</u> woman <u>shouted</u>.

A Hey

B back

C surprised

D shouted

9 Which of the underlined words is NOT a preposition?

> Because <u>of</u> the verdict presented <u>by</u> the jury, the three defendants will <u>all</u> be going <u>to</u> jail.

A of   **B** by   **C** all   **D** to

10 Which type of conjunction is the underlined group of words?

> <u>Neither</u> Tommy <u>nor</u> Angela has detention this afternoon.

A not conjunctions   **C** correlative

B coordinating   **D** subordinating

11 **Which emotion does the underlined interjection display?**

> <u>Ouch</u>! Tammy hit her head on the pavement when she fell off her bicycle.

A joy

B pain

C surprise

D dismay

12 **Which of the underlined words is a preposition?**

> <u>There</u> <u>should</u> not be any animosity <u>between</u> the <u>two</u> teams.

A There

B should

C between

D two

13 **Which of the underlined words is a conjunction?**

> Shineka <u>and</u> Marcelle <u>love</u> <u>to</u> eat jellybeans before <u>dinner</u>.

A and

B love

C to

D dinner

14 **Which of the underlined words is a preposition?**

> I need to <u>make</u> a decision <u>about</u> where I <u>want</u> to <u>attend</u> summer school.

A make

B about

C want

D attend

15 **Which of the underlined words is NOT a conjunction?**

> Marjorie <u>and</u> Bryan need to <u>study</u> for Spanish <u>when</u> they get home today <u>because</u> they have a test tomorrow.

A and

B study

C when

D because

16 **Choose the appropriate interjection for the feeling shown in the parentheses.**

> (Surprise)! Jordan just blew the biggest bubble I've ever seen!

A Stop

B Oh no

C Well

D Wow

17 **What type of conjunction is the underlined word?**

> In the mornings, I make freshly squeezed orange juice, <u>but</u> Janice prefers milk.

A not a conjunction

B coordinating

C correlative

D subordinating

18 **Which of the underlined words is the object of the preposition _in_?**

> Flannery O'Connor lived in <u>Milledgeville</u> <u>until</u> she <u>died</u> at <u>age</u> thirty-nine.

A Milledgeville

B until

C died

D age

19 Which emotion does the underlined interjection display?

"<u>Alas</u>, poor Yorick! I knew him," said Hamlet.

A joy

B surprise

C pity

D impatience

20 How many conjunctions are in the following sentence?

I have often wondered about the career I will have when I grow up, but I can never seem to come to a conclusion.

A one

B two

C three

D four

21 Which of the underlined words is NOT used as a preposition?

<u>Before</u> Georgette goes <u>to</u> work, she stops <u>at</u> the café <u>for</u> coffee.

A Before

B to

C at

D for

22 Which interjection would best fill in the blank?

_____! What a great idea!

A Ouch

B Oh no

C Hey

D Well

23 Which of the underlined words is a subordinating conjunction?

> Although the prosecutor had some valid points, the jury found the defendant not guilty.

A Although

B points

C found

D guilty

24 Which word is the object of the underlined preposition?

> As the rhyme goes, "In 1492, Columbus sailed the ocean blue."

A rhyme

B 1492

C Columbus

D ocean

25 Which type of conjunction is the underlined word?

> Ryan never remembers to do his homework, and his teacher always scolds him.

A. not a conjunction

B. coordinating

C. correlative

D. subordinating

Chapter 7
Sentence Structure

This chapter addresses the following GPS-based CRCT standard:

ELA6C1	The student demonstrates understanding and control of the rules of the English language, realizing that usage involves the appropriate application of conventions and grammar in both written and spoken formats. The student
	b. Recognizes basic parts of a sentence (subject, verb, direct object, indirect object, predicate noun, predicate adjective).
	c. Identifies and writes simple, compound, complex, and compound-complex sentences, avoiding fragments and run-ons.

What is your favorite way to communicate? Is it by texting your friends, writing notes, talking, or some other way? Communicating has a structure. Words build sentences. Sentences build paragraphs. Paragraphs build larger works of writing.

In this chapter, you will practice grammar rules that will help you to be a better reader and writer. **Sentence structure** is the main focus. Sentence structure is how sentences are put together. There are some basic elements in every sentence. We will begin with a look at the two main sentence elements—the subject and predicate.

SUBJECT AND PREDICATE

A **subject** tells whom or what the sentence is about. A **predicate** tells something about the subject. A complete subject or predicate may consist of one word. It may also be more than one word. Here are some examples.

Misty / went to her grandmother's house.
subject   **predicate**

In this sentence, the complete subject is *Misty,* because the sentence is about Misty. She performs the action of the sentence. The complete predicate is *went to her grandmother's house.* This tells the reader something about Misty. Let's take a look at another example.

Nine students / forgot to bring in permission slips.
subject   **predicate**

In this sentence, the complete subject is *nine students.* The complete predicate is *forgot to bring in permission slips.*

Practice 1: Subject and Predicate
6C1b

Read each of the following sentences. Choose whether the underlined part is the subject or the predicate.

> <u>Carrots</u> are a healthy snack.

1. The underlined part of this sentence is the

    A. subject.   B. predicate.

> Beans and rice <u>are a good nutritional combination.</u>

2. The underlined part of this sentence is the
    A. subject.   B. predicate.

> <u>House plants</u> help to maintain indoor air quality.

3. The underlined part of this sentence is the
    A. subject.   B. predicate.

> <u>Summer camp</u> is one exciting option for spending summer vacation time.

4. The underlined part of this sentence is the
    A. subject.   B. predicate.

> There are many types of domestic animals.

5. The underlined part of this sentence is the
   A. subject.   B. predicate.

In the examples above, you identified **simple and complete subjects and predicates**. Let's take a look at some more examples of subjects and predicates. This time, we will look for simple subjects and simple predicates.

Her cheerful soccer teammates / screamed all the way to the ice cream parlor.
        subject   **predicate**

The complete subject of this sentence would be *Her cheerful soccer teammates*. This is the main idea of the sentence. The main word here is *teammates*, so *teammates* would be the **simple subject**. One way to identify the simple subject is to think of simplifying a sentence. What words could you eliminate and still have the same idea? In this case, if you dropped *her cheerful soccer*, you would still retain the word *teammates*, which is the key to the main idea of the sentence. Let's look at the predicate of this sentence and identify the simple predicate.

...screamed all the way to the ice cream parlor.

In this part of the sentence, the main word is *screamed*. If we took away the other words—*all the way to the ice cream parlor*—the meaning of the sentence would still be the same. However, without this word, *screamed*, the meaning of the sentence would change. In this way we know that s*creamed* is the **simple predicate** of this sentence. It is the main word that states the action of the sentence.

When you identify the simple predicate, look for the verb or the verb phrase. A **verb phrase** consists of the main verb and its helping verbs.

Example: The little ones have gone to bed.

In this sentence, *have gone* (main verb *gone* plus helping verb *have*) is the verb phrase. This is the simple subject.

Practice 2:   Simple Subjects and Predicates
6C1b

Read each sentence, and choose the correct answer to the questions that follow.

> The heavy downpour would not subside.

1. What is the simple subject in this sentence?
   A. the heavy downpour   C. downpour
   B. would not subside   D. subside

2. What is the simple predicate in this sentence?
   A. the heavy downpour
   C. downpour
   B. would subside
   D. subside

> Jeans are comfortable clothing.

3. What is the simple subject in this sentence?
   A. jeans
   B. you
   C. jeans are
   D. none of these

4. Which one of the following is the simple predicate in the sentence?
   A. are
   C. are comfortable
   B. comfortable
   D. jeans

PREDICATE NOMINATIVES AND PREDICATE ADJECTIVES

There are many ways to arrange words in a sentence. In previous chapters, you learned about parts of speech. You also took a look at how various parts of speech might be used in a sentence. In this chapter, you will look at some special functions for nouns, pronouns, and adjectives in a sentence. You will learn to identify predicate nominatives and predicate adjectives.

A **predicate nominative** is a noun or pronoun that follows a linking verb. It identifies the subject of the verb or refers to it. Let's look at some examples.

My best friend is a <u>Labrador</u>.

In this sentence, *Labrador* is a predicate nominative. It is a noun that identifies *best friend*. Here is another example.

The coat on the table is <u>hers</u>.

In this sentence, *hers* is a predicate nominative. It is a pronoun that identifies *coat*.

A **predicate adjective** is an adjective that follows a linking verb and describes the subject.

Example 1: Marcia feels <u>groggy</u>.

In this sentence, *groggy* is an adjective that follows the linking verb *feels*. It describes *Marcia*. Here is another example.

Example 2: Her teeth are so <u>white</u>.

White is an adjective that follows the linking verb *are*. It describes *teeth*.

Practice 3: Predicate Nominatives and Predicate Adjectives
6C1b

Read each sentence, and follow the directions.

> Carmen is one of the greatest dancers.

1. In this sentence, what is the function of the word *dancers*?

    A. predicate adjective

    B. predicate noun

    C. predicate pronoun

    D. both A and B

> Strawberry ice cream is so very yummy.

2. In this sentence, the predicate adjective is

    A. strawberry.   B. yummy.   C. so.   D. ice cream.

> Brownies are a great snack.

3. In this sentence, the word *snack* is a

    A. predicate.   C. predicate noun.

    B. subject.   D. predicate adjective.

> Cupcakes are great!

4. In this sentence, the word *great* is a

    A. predicate.   C. predicate noun.

    B. subject.   D. predicate adjective.

DIRECT AND INDIRECT OBJECTS

In this section, you will learn about special jobs of nouns and pronouns in a sentence. These words can function as direct objects and indirect objects. Let's first take a look at direct objects.

DIRECT OBJECTS

A **direct object** is a noun or pronoun that receives the action of the verb or shows the result of the action. A direct object tells whom or what after an action verb. For example:

> I took my *dress* to the cleaners.

In this sentence, the verb is *took*. If you ask yourself what was taken, then the response should be *dress*. The dress was taken to the cleaners. *Dress* is the direct object. Let's look at another example.

> Maria wanted *icing* on the cake.

In this sentence, *wanted* is the verb. If you ask yourself what Maria wanted, the response should be *icing*. Maria wanted icing. *Icing* is the direct object.

INDIRECT OBJECTS

An **indirect object** is a noun or pronoun that comes between the action verb and the direct object. It tells to what or to whom the action of the verb is done. It also tells for what or for whom the action of the verb is done. Here are some examples.

> Spencer gave the angry *bully* half of his lunch.

In this sentence, the noun *bully* tells to whom Spencer gave half of his lunch. *Bully* is the indirect object. Here is another example:

> Laina loaned *Jena* two dollars to buy stickers at the book fair.

In this sentence, the noun *Jena* tells to whom Laina loaned two dollars. *Jena* is the indirect object.

Practice 4: Direct and Indirect Objects
6C1b

Read each sentence, and choose the best answer to the questions.

> We took votes for the new class president.

1. In this sentence, which of the following is the direct object?

   A. We took votes

   B. votes

   C. new class president

   D. none of these

> Dominique shared cupcakes with the sixth grade class.

2. In this sentence, which of the following is the direct object?
   A. Dominique
   B. shared cupcakes
   C. cupcakes
   D. none of these

> My language arts teacher gave us a pop quiz on spelling words.

3. In this sentence, which of the following is the indirect object?
   A. us
   B. language arts teacher
   C. spelling words
   D. none of these

> Birva showed her friends the new iPod she received as a birthday present.

4. In this sentence, which of the following is the indirect object?
   A. iPod
   B. present
   C. friends
   D. none of these

TYPES OF SENTENCES

Understanding sentence structures is a part of being a good reader. Sentence structure means the way a sentence is formed. In this section, you will take a look at four sentence types. They are simple, compound, complex, and compound-complex sentences. We will begin with a look at simple sentences.

SIMPLE SENTENCES

A **simple sentence** is just as the term suggests—simple. A simple sentence has one independent clause and no subordinate clauses. Let's take a look at some simple sentences.

> An independent clause can stand alone as a sentence. It expresses a complete thought. A subordinate clause can't stand alone as a sentence because it doesn't express a complete thought.

Examples: Mario went to the school Fall Harvest Dance.

Jillian took notes during the social studies lecture.

These are sentences, as they express complete thoughts. There are no subordinate clauses.

A simple sentence may contain compound structures such as compound subjects, compound verbs, or even both.

Example: Mario and Jillian went to the school Fall Harvest Dance.

This is a simple sentence with a compound subject, *Mario and Jillian.*

Example: Jillian took notes and did homework during the social studies lecture.

This is a simple sentence with a compound verb, *took notes and did homework.*

COMPOUND SENTENCES

A **compound sentence** is made up of independent clauses. There are two or more independent clauses in a compound sentence. Remember that each independent clause is a complete sentence that can stand alone. In compound sentences, coordinating conjunctions (*for, and, nor, but, or, yet, so*) are used between clauses.

Example: Eugene likes to play baseball, *and* he enjoys participating in the school anime club.

Notice that in this sentence, there are two clauses that could stand alone:

Eugene likes to play baseball.

He enjoys participating in the school anime club.

The conjunction *and* joins the clauses together. Here is another example.

Harvey doesn't do his daily chores, *but* he does usually complete his homework.

Independent clause one: Harvey doesn't do his daily chores.

Independent clause two: He does usually complete his homework.

Coordinating conjunction: but

COMPLEX SENTENCES

A **complex sentence** has one independent clause. It also has at least one subordinate clause. Let's take a look at some examples:

As Katelyn flipped through the glossy pages of the magazine, she spotted an outfit that was a "must-have."

In this sentence, the second part of the sentence is an independent clause. It expresses a complete thought, and it could stand alone:

She spotted an outfit that was a "must-have."

The first part of the sentence is a subordinate clause. It does not express a complete thought. It cannot stand alone.

As Katelyn flipped through the glossy pages of the magazine…

Here is another example.

Many middle school students enjoy chatting with friends while eating lunch.

Independent clause: Many middle school students enjoy chatting with friends.

Subordinate clause: while eating lunch

COMPOUND-COMPLEX SENTENCES

The **compound-complex sentence** combines parts of the compound sentence with parts of the complex sentence. It has two or more independent clauses. It also has at least one subordinate clause. Let's take a look at some examples.

Before I go to bed each night, I call my friends for a gossip update, but they are usually not allowed to talk on the phone at night.

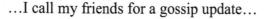

Let's dissect this sentence structure:

Before I go to bed each night...

This does not express a complete thought. It is a subordinate clause.

...I call my friends for a gossip update...

This is an independent clause. It expresses a complete thought.

...but...

This is a coordinating conjunction. It is used to join two independent clauses.

...they are usually not allowed to talk on the phone at night.

This is an independent clause. It expresses a complete thought.

Compound-complex sentences can be challenging. As you can see, if we break it down into sections, then we see the parts that make it up. Let's try another example.

The halls cleared quickly as Mr. O'Connor did his usual sixth-period sweep, but a few students straggled as they scrambled through messy lockers and tried to get to class.

Independent Clauses: The halls cleared quickly...a few students straggled...

Subordinate Clauses

...as Mr. O'Connor did his usual sixth-period sweep...

...as they scrambled though messy lockers...

...tried to get to class.

Coordinating Conjunctions: ...but...and...

Practice 5:   Types of Sentences
6C1c

Read each sentence. Decide if the sentence is simple, compound, complex, or compound-complex. Choose the letter of the sentence structure type that matches your choice.

1. Dallas likes to dance, but she is very picky about her music.

    A. simple

    B. compound

    C. complex

    D. compound-complex

2. Chase has only been playing the viola since fourth grade, and as an eighth grader, he is already one of the best in the state.
   A. simple
   C. complex
   B. compound
   D. compound-complex

3. When I have a lot of homework, I like to start with my hardest subject.
   A. simple
   B. compound
   C. complex
   D. compound-complex

   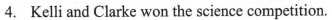

4. Kelli and Clarke won the science competition.
   A. simple
   C. complex
   B. compound
   D. compound-complex

5. Before my stepmom opened the oven, I could smell the fresh pizza baking, and I got hungry.
   A. simple
   C. complex
   B. compound
   D. compound-complex

6. Tyrone lives near the beach, so he goes fishing almost every weekend.
   A. simple
   C. complex
   B. compound
   D. compound-complex

CHAPTER 7 SUMMARY

A sentence has two parts: a **subject** and a **predicate**. A subject tells whom or what the sentence is about. A predicate tells something about the subject.

A **predicate nominative** is a noun or pronoun that follows a linking verb and identifies its subject or refers to it.

A **predicate adjective** is an adjective that follows a linking verb and describes the subject.

A **direct object is** a noun or pronoun that receives the action of the verb or shows the result of the action. A direct object tells whom or what after an action verb.

An **indirect object** is a noun or pronoun that comes between the action verb and the direct object, and tells to what or to whom or for what or for whom the action of the verb is done.

A **simple sentence** has one independent clause and no subordinate clauses.

A **compound sentence** has two or more independent clauses but no subordinate clauses. Coordinating conjunctions (*for, and, nor, but, or, yet, so*) are often used to join independent clauses.

A **complex sentence** has one independent clause and at least one subordinate clause.

A **compound-complex sentence** has two or more independent clauses and at least one subordinate clause.

CHAPTER 7 REVIEW

6C1b, c

For 1–4, decide which choice correctly separates the subject and predicate in each sentence.

1 **A** I / have many assignments due next week.

   B I have / many assignments due next week.

   C I have many / assignments due next week.

   D none of these

2 **A** There are nine members / of my girl scout troop.

   B There are / nine members of my girl scout troop.

   C There are nine / members of my girl scout troop.

   D none of these

3 **A** Maria's family will / vacation at the beach.

   B Maria's family will vacation / at the beach.

   C Maria's family / will vacation at the beach.

   D none of these

4 **A** I / want to be a singer someday.

   B I want / to be a singer someday.

   C I want to be / a singer someday.

   D none of these

For 5–8, choose the word that is the predicate noun in each sentence.

5 **My favorite dessert is ice cream.**
   A favorite   **B** ice cream   **C** dessert   **D** none of these

6 **The final answer was "1986".**
   A final   **B** answer   **C** 1986   **D** none of these

7 **Shauna's mother is a nurse.**
   A Shauna's   **B** mother   **C** nurse   **D** none of these

8   The hairy pig was so very cute.
   A. cute   **B** very   **C** pig   **D** none of these

For 9–12, choose the word that is the predicate adjective in each sentence.

9   My favorite ice cream flavor is chocolate.
   A favorite   **B** ice cream   **C** chocolate   **D** none of these

10   The hurricane's wind was strong.
   A hurricane's   **B** strong   **C** wind   **D** none of these

11   The air on the beach was cold and windy.
   A cold   **B** windy   **C** both A and B   **D** none of these

12   Baby Ella's hair is cute and curly.
   A hair   **B** cute   **C** curly   **D** both B and C

For 13–16, identify the direct object in each sentence.

13   Shelly put her jacket on the plastic hanger.

   A Shelly

   B jacket

   C plastic hanger

   D none of these

14   My aunt collects stamps.

   A aunt

   B collects

   C my

   D stamps

15   The custodian collected bags of party day garbage.

   A custodian

   B bags

   C party day

   D garbage

16   The official announced the results of the controversial play.

   A official

   B results

C play

D none of these

For 17–20, identify the indirect object in each sentence.

17 The stylist gave me a trendy bob.

    A stylist   **B** trendy   **C** me   **D** none of these

18 The nanny gave the crying toddler a toy.

    A toddler

    B toy

    C nanny

    D none of these

19 Ms. Parker bought her homeroom students donuts to celebrate their exemplary test scores.

    A Ms. Parker

    B students

    C test

    D none of these

20 After a fun day at the beach, the relaxed mom gave her family a fun dinner of pizza and hot dogs.

    A dinner

    B pizza

    C family

    D none of these

For 21–25, decide if the sentence structures are simple, compound, complex, or compound-complex.

21 Louis and Nigel have been best friends since they met in the first grade.

    A simple

    B complex

    C compound

    D compound-complex

22 The technician did an X-ray for the swallowed key, but, as he searched, he found nothing unusual in the dog's digestive tract.

   A simple

   B compound

   C complex

   D compound-complex

23 You could go to bed now or later.

   A simple

   B complex

   C compound

   D compound-complex

24 I will have peanut butter and jelly for lunch, and I will have spaghetti for dinner.

   A simple

   B complex

   C compound

   D compound-complex

25 Jessica wanted to go to bed, but she still had work to do.

   A simple

   B complex

   C compound

   D compound-complex

Chapter 8
Fragments and Run-ons

This chapter addresses the following GPS-based CRCT standards:

ELA6C1	The student demonstrates understanding and control of the rules of the English language, realizing that usage involves the appropriate application of conventions and grammar in both written and spoken formats. The student
	c. Identifies and writes simple, compound, complex, and compound-complex sentences, avoiding fragments and run-ons.
	d. Demonstrates appropriate comma and semicolon usage (compound and complex sentences, appositives, words in direct address).

In chapter 7, we discussed types of sentences. This chapter also deals with sentences, but the focus is sentence problems. Two major sentence problems are **fragments** and **run-ons**. A fragment occurs when a group of words that was meant to stand alone as a sentence does not express a complete thought. A run-on happens when two or more sentences are fused together without the use of proper punctuation. Let's look at each of these types of sentence errors.

FRAGMENTS

Do you have a friend who likes to tell stories but always omits a key detail? Listening to the story, you can't really understand it all or get the full picture. **Fragments** are similar to this. Fragments are word groups that were intended to be sentences but do not make sense. There is something left out that makes the sentence fail as a complete thought. There may be no subject or no predicate. The problem with fragments is similar to the problem of a friend that tells an incomplete story. The word groups fail to communicate a full idea. Let's look at some fragment examples.

The dog's toy.

What about the dog's toy? This makes no sense. This group of words lacks a predicate. What if we add a predicate? We get: The dog's toy *is in his crate*. This group of words expresses a complete thought. The addition of a predicate to the word group completes the sentence.

Let's take a look at another example.

In the car.

This group of words lacks a subject. Who or what is in the car? This group of words lacks a subject. If we add a subject, then we get, "My sweat shirt is in the car." This group of words expresses a complete thought. It is a sentence.

Practice 1: Fragments
6C1c

A Decide if each word group is a sentence or a fragment.

B If it is a fragment, use your own paper to add a subject or predicate to make it a complete sentence. Share your new sentence with a partner.

1. The birds sang sweetly.

    A. sentence   B. fragment

2. The sweet birds.

    A. sentence   B. fragment

3. My favorite candies are jellybeans.

    A. sentence   B. fragment

4. Are jellybeans?

    A. sentence   B. fragment

5. Are jellybeans your favorite candies?

    A. sentence   B. fragment

RUN-ONS

When two or more complete sentences are fused together without the proper punctuation, you get a **run-on**. Run-ons make writing unclear. A reader can become confused about where one idea ends and another begins.

You can think of run-ons as similar to streets without stop signs or stop lights. This would cause a horrible mess. In the same way, run-on sentences create a mess of confusion for the reader.

To revise a run-on sentence, a writer may do one of the following:

- Make two separate sentences.
- Use a comma and an appropriate coordinating conjunction.
- Use a semicolon; when you use a semicolon, you do not use a coordinating conjunction.

COORDINATING CONJUNCTIONS

for

and

nor

but

or

yet

so

Let's take a look at some examples of run-ons.

My friends like to play Uno they don't like to watch television.

This word group includes two separate sentences that are not properly punctuated.

Sentence one: My friends like to play Uno.

Sentence two: They don't like to watch television.

One way to correct the run-on would be to separate it into the two sentences that combined to make it. This is what has been done above. But what if you want to keep the ideas together? After all, you're trying to make the point that your friends would rather play Uno than watch television. There are two ways to do this.

Add a comma and a coordinating conjunction:

Example: My friends like to play Uno, **but** they don't like to watch television.

Add a semicolon:

Example: My friends like to play Uno; they don't like to watch television.

Here is another example.

> Sarah and Connie are great friends they have known each other since the very first gymnastics class in third grade.

Separate the run-on into two sentences:

> **Example:** Sarah and Connie are great friends. They have known each other since the very first gymnastics class in third grade.

or

Add a comma and a coordinating conjunction:

> **Example:** Sarah and Connie are great friends, **as** they have known each other since the very first gymnastics class in third grade.

or

Add a semicolon:

> **Example:** Sarah and Connie are great friends; they have known each other since the very first gymnastics class in third grade.

Practice 2: Run-ons
6C1c, d

Read each example. Decide which version is written correctly, avoiding run-on errors.

1. A. The party for my twelfth birthday will be at my grandmother's house she makes the best birthday cakes.

   B. The party for my twelfth birthday will be at my grandmother's house. She makes the best birthday cakes.

   C. The party for my twelfth birthday will be at my grandmother's house, she makes the best birthday cakes.

   D. The party for my twelfth birthday will be at my grandmother's house; because she makes the best birthday cakes.

2. A. Penelope and Dawn ate brownies and played Monopoly they had a fun Friday night slumber party.

   B. Penelope and Dawn ate brownies and played Monopoly, they had a fun Friday night slumber party.

   C. Penelope and Dawn ate brownies and played Monopoly; they had a fun Friday night slumber party.

   D. Penelope and Dawn ate brownies and played Monopoly, nor they had a fun Friday night slumber party.

3. A. The students will celebrate the rise to seventh grade with a sixth grade pep rally there will be many fun activities and an outside barbecue.

    B. The students will celebrate the rise to seventh grade with a sixth grade pep rally; there will be many fun activities and an outside barbecue.

    C. The students will celebrate the rise to seventh grade with a sixth grade pep rally, there will be many fun activities and an outside barbecue.

    D. The students will celebrate the rise to seventh grade with a sixth grade pep rally, yet there will be many fun activities and an outside barbecue.

4. A. Charles likes to read books and do artwork he is a member of the school Book Talk group.

    B. Charles likes to read books and do artwork and he is a member of the school Book Talk group.

    C. Charlie likes to read books and do artwork; but he is a member of the school Book Talk group.

    D. Charlie likes to read books and do artwork, and he is a member of the school Book Talk group.

CHAPTER 8 SUMMARY

Fragments are word groups that were intended to be sentences but lack either a subject or predicate. Fragments fail to communicate a full idea.

When two complete sentences are fused together without proper punctuation, the result is a run-on. **Run-ons** make writing unclear. A reader becomes confused about where one idea ends and another begins.

Don't Forget!

CHAPTER 8 REVIEW
6C1c, d

For questions 1–10, decide if the word groups are sentences or fragments.

1 Ana and Marie, friends from church.

   A sentence   **B** fragment

2 Bobbi will travel to the coast to visit her hometown.

   A sentence   **B** fragment

3 Will you take me?

   A sentence   **B** fragment

4 Can't you go to the store before you go to the gym?

   A sentence   **B** fragment

5 Julia's designer jeans, expensive but simple.

   A sentence   **B** fragment

6 Who are you?

   A sentence   **B** fragment

7 Don't go to the park alone.

   A sentence   **B** fragment

8 My friends' likes and dislikes.

   A sentence   **B** fragment

9 Will there be plenty of activities at the county fair?

   A sentence   **B** fragment

10 Please put the books away.

   A sentence   **B** fragment

For questions 11–15, decide which word group is written correctly, avoiding run-ons.

11 **A** I ate pizza, hot dogs, and ice cream, and the combination gave me an upset stomach.

B I ate pizza, hot dogs, and ice cream, the combination gave me an upset stomach.

C I ate pizza, hot dogs, and ice cream, when the combination gave me an upset stomach.

D I ate pizza, hot dogs, and ice cream and the combination gave me an upset stomach.

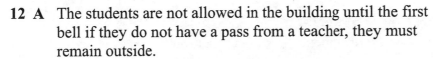

12 **A** The students are not allowed in the building until the first bell if they do not have a pass from a teacher, they must remain outside.

B The students are not allowed in the building until the first bell; if they do not have a pass from a teacher, they must remain outside.

C The students are not allowed in the building. Until the first bell if they do not have a pass from a teacher, they must remain outside.

D The students are not allowed in the building until the first bell; and if they do not have a pass from a teacher, they must remain outside.

13 **A** I will not go to the math help session if my friend Carrie will not be there her mother always gives me a ride home.

B I will not go to the math help session if my friend Carrie will not be there, so her mother always gives me a ride home.

C I will not go to the math help session if my friend Carrie will not be there; her mother always gives me a ride home.

D I will not go to the math help session. If my friend Carrie will not be there her mother always gives me a ride home.

14 **A** Will you go to the mall with me, I need to buy shoes for soccer?

B Will you go to the mall with me? I need to buy shoes for soccer.

C Will you go to the mall with me. I need to buy shoes for soccer.

D Will you go to the mall with me; I need to buy shoes for soccer?

15 **A** My cousin will visit the country this winter. She is from Italy.

    B My cousin will visit the country this winter she is from Italy.

    C My cousin. Will visit the country this winter. She is from Italy.

    D My cousin will visit the country this winter, she is from Italy.

For questions 16–19, decide whether each example is a sentence, a fragment, or a run-on.

16 **I am keeping track of all the books I read this summer my English teacher will want to see a list.**
    A sentence   **B** fragment   **C** run-on

17 **The same jacket that Sam wears.**
    A sentence   **B** fragment   **C** run-on

18 **That time, she didn't get the ball back to the base, and the runner was safe.**

    A sentence

    B fragment

    C run-on

19 **The broccoli, peas, and other vegetables you don't like to eat.**
    A sentence   **B** fragment   **C** run-on

20 **Revise any fragments or run-ons you found in questions 16–19, so that they are complete and correctly punctuated sentences.**

Chapter 9
Spelling

This chapter addresses the following GPS-based CRCT standards:

ELA6C1	The student demonstrates understanding and control of the rules of the English language, realizing that usage involves the appropriate application of conventions and grammar in both written and spoken formats. The student
	e. Uses common spelling rules, applies common spelling patterns, and develops and masters words that are commonly misspelled.
	f. Produces final drafts that demonstrate accurate spelling and the correct use of punctuation and capitalization.
ELA6W2	The student demonstrates competence in a variety of genres.
	The student produces **technical** writing (friendly letters, thank-you notes, formula poems, instructions) that:
	d. Applies rules of Standard English.
ELA6W4	The student consistently uses the writing process to develop, revise, and evaluate writing. The student
	c. Edits to correct errors in spelling, punctuation, etc.

HOW WELL DO YOU SPELL?

"Take care that you never spell a word wrong. Always, before you write a word, consider how it is spelled, and, if you do not remember, turn to a dictionary."

– Thomas Jefferson

Spelling well is not easy. After all, our language has more than a thousand ways to spell forty-four different sounds. It is a language in which the words "Halloween" and "Tangerine" rhyme, but "woven" and "oven" do not.

You don't have to win the National Spelling Bee to think of yourself as a good speller. But you will need a couple of tricks and a few rules.

Good spelling skills can be learned—it just takes determination and lots of practice. As you read, make a list of words that are new to you. Write down their correct spelling and meaning. When you misspell a word, add it to the list and underline the part of the word that you got wrong.

Try to learn a new word every day. Use these words in sentences. Practice spelling them over and over. Gradually, pictures of correctly spelled words will form in your mind. And when you see a word that is *not* spelled correctly, it will set off an alarm.

singal   signal   signel

(Which word set off your "wrong" alarm?)

Tips for Better Spelling	
1 **Proofread.**	Carefully proofread your written work to find errors.
2 **Keep a list.**	Use a notebook to record the words you misspell. Write the correct spelling next to your mistake.
3 **Underline.**	Place a line under the part of the word that you missed. **Wrong** **Right** **Example:** desp<u>a</u>rate desperate
4 **Learn one word at a time.**	Don't take on a whole bunch. Try to learn one new word a day, along with its meaning. Write it in your notebook.
5 **Use your new words in sentences.**	
6 **Practice, practice, practice.**	

SPELLING RULES

Here are some spelling rules to remember. Let's start with some rules for making a word longer by adding to it.

ADDING SUFFIXES

When you want to extend a word by adding a suffix, follow these instructions:

Rule: If a suffix begins with a consonant like *-ment, -ness, -less, -ful*, keep the final *-e* of the root word.

    Examples: pronounce = pronouncement; peace = peaceful

Rule: If a one-syllable word ends in a consonant with a single vowel before it, like *fan* or *slip*, double the consonant before adding *-ing*.

    Examples: fan = fanning; slip = slipping

Rule: If a word has more than one syllable and ends in a single consonant preceded by a single vowel, like beg*in,* double the consonant before adding *-ed* or *-ing*.

Examples: begin = beginning; refer = referred

Practice 1: Adding Suffixes
6C1e, f, 6W2tech.d, 6W4c

Use the rules you just learned to answer the following questions.

1. Which word is spelled correctly?

   A. sliping   B. pavment   C. controlling   D. likness

2. Which word is NOT spelled correctly?

   A. taning   B. preferring   C. joyful   D. defining

3. Which word is spelled correctly?

   A. forcful   B. kidnaped   C. trimming   D. retirment

WORDS ENDING IN *CE* OR *J* SOUNDS OR DOUBLE VOWELS

Here are some rules for a few tricky words. When you use these, write the correct spelling in your notebook. Try to memorize the words that follow these rules:

Rule: If a word ending in *ce* has a soft sound, like *s,* keep the final *e* before adding a suffix.

    Example: replace = replaceable

Rule: If a word ends in *ge* and has a *j* sound, like "change," keep the final *e* before adding a suffix.

    Example: change = changeable

Rule: If a word ends in two vowels (vowel + final *e*), keep the final vowel before adding a suffix.

    Examples: shoe = shoeing; see = seeable

Practice 2: Words Ending in *ce* or *j* Sounds or Double Vowels
6C1e, f, 6W2tech.d, 6W4c

Use the rules you just learned to answer the following questions.

1. Which word is spelled correctly?

   A. fleing   B. noticable   C. strangness   D. arrangement

2. Which word is NOT spelled correctly?

   A. canoeing   B. peaceable   C. couragous   D. changeable

THE *I* BEFORE *E* RULE

Learn and follow this rule to improve your spelling. You will use it a lot, so memorize this poem:

Rule: *i* before *e* except after *c*

   Or when sounding like *a*

   As in "**neighbor**" and "**weigh**."

Practice 3: The *i* before *e* Rule
6C1e, f, 6W2tech.d, 6W4c

Use the rule you just learned to answer the following questions.

1. Which word is spelled correctly?
   A. cheif   B. friend   C. frieght   D. beleive

2. Which word is NOT spelled correctly?
   A. piece   B. niece   C. recieve   D. receipt

3. Which word is spelled correctly?
   A. hieght   B. grieve   C. releive   D. decieve

There are some exceptions. When *c* is pronounced *sh*, use *ie*.

   Examples: conscience, sufficient

And there are many words that just don't follow the rules. These outlaws include *height, sleight, leisure, forfeit,* and others. When you run into an outlaw word, it will help to write it on a 3 x 5 card and memorize it.

REGULAR SPELLING

Most nouns can be made plural by adding *-s*. (book = books; elephant = elephants).

Most regular verbs simply add *-ed* and *-ing* to the base form (listen, listened, listening).

But there are some variations.

IRREGULAR PLURAL FORMATIONS OF NOUNS

Rule: For nouns that end in *-s, -x, -z, -sh,* or *-ch,* add *-es* to make them plural.

> **Examples:** recess = recesses; tax = taxes;
> fish = fishes; match = matches.

Rule: For nouns that end in *-f* or *-fe,* change the *-f* to *-v* and add *-es*.

> **Examples:** self = selves; wife = wives.

Rule: For nouns that end in *-o,* add *-es*.

> **Examples:** tomato = tomatoes; veto = vetoes.

Certain exceptions, such as *piano/pianos, zoo/zoos, solo/solos,* are ones you can add to your list of words to learn. Then, you can memorize their spelling.

Practice 4: Irregular Plural Formations of Nouns
6C1e, f, 6W2tech.d, 6W4c

Use the rules you learned about irregular forms to answer the following questions.

1. Which word is spelled correctly?
   A. heros   B. peachs   C. buzzes   D. knifes

2. Which word is spelled correctly?
   A. elfs   B. rashs   C. sandwichs   D. brushes

3. Which word is NOT spelled correctly?
   A. boxes   B. shelves   C. potatos   D. crutches

IRREGULAR SPELLING OF VERBS

Rule: With many verbs, adding *-s, -ed,* or *-ing* will not change the verb form.

> **Examples:** hit = hits, hitting; view = views, viewed, viewing.

But for some verbs, changes must be made.

Rule: If the verb ends in a *silent e,* drop the *e* before adding *-ing* or *-ed.*

> **Examples:** bake = baking; smile = smiled, smiling

Rule: With *ie* or *ee* endings, drop the final *e* before adding *-ed.*

> **Examples:** lie = lied; free = freed.

Practice 5: Irregular Spelling of Verbs
6C1e, f, 6W2tech.d, 6W4c

Now use the rules you learned to answer the following questions.

1. Which word is spelled correctly?
   - A. refereede
   - B. blaming
   - C. decideed
   - D. shakeing

2. Which word is spelled correctly?
   - A. listed
   - B. jumpng
   - C. throwes
   - D. traineng

3. Which word is NOT spelled correctly?
   - A. dyed
   - B. rated
   - C. debating
   - D. restoreing

OTHER VERB ENDINGS

Rule: If the word ends in *-s, -x, -z, -ch,* or *-sh*, you add *-e* before the *-s* ending.

> **Examples:** toss = tosses; mix = mixes; push = pushes; reach = reaches

Rule: To add *-ed* to a word ending in *-y*, change *-y* to *-i*, then add *-ed*.

> **Examples:** cry = cried; marry = married.

Rule: To add -s to a word ending in *-y*, change the *-y* to *-ie*.

> **Examples:** vary = varies; fry = fries.

Rule: *But* if the base form has an *-ie* ending, change *-ie* to *-y* before adding *-ing*.

> **Examples:** die = dying; tie = tying.

Practice 6: Other Verb Endings
6C1e, f, 6W2tech.d, 6W4c

Now use these rules to answer the following questions.

1. Which word is spelled correctly?
   - A. fixs
   - B. crashs
   - C. hurrys
   - D. preaches

2. Which word is NOT spelled correctly?
   - A. tried
   - B. carried
   - C. betrayng
   - D. tallying

3. Which word is spelled correctly?
   - A. catchs
   - B. clases
   - C. dollying
   - D. implieng

COMMON SPELLING PATTERNS

Sounds can be spelled in many ways. For example, the long *a* sound can be spelled as it is in *way* or *weigh*. Both sound the same.

Let's look at some letters and the various ways their sounds can be spelled.

The Letter A

a = stay   ai = rain   eigh = eight

ay at the end of a word, as in *pray*

ey at the end of a word, as in *they*

Practice 7: The Letter A
6C1e, f, 6W2tech.d, 6W4c

Select the correct letters to fill in the blanks and make a complete word.

1. pl___
   - A. a
   - B. ai
   - C. ay
   - D. ey

2. st___n
   - A. a
   - B. ai
   - C. ay
   - D. ey

3. fr___med
   - A. a
   - B. ai
   - C. ay
   - D. ey

The Letter O

o = row   au = beau   ew = sew   ough = though

Practice 8: The Letter O
6C1e, f, 6W2tech.d, 6W4c

Select the correct letters to fill in the blanks and make a complete word.

1. b___ne
   - A. o
   - B. ew
   - C. au
   - D. ough

2. fl___
   - A. o
   - B. ow
   - C. au
   - D. ew

3. expl___de
   - A. o
   - B. ew
   - C. ow
   - D. ough

The Letter U
u = blue   oo = room   ew = grew   ough = through

Practice 9: The Letter U
6C1e, f, 6W2tech.d, 6W4c

Select the correct letters to fill in the blanks and make a complete word.

1. z___m
    A. u   B. oo   C. ew   D. ough

2. fl___te
    A. u   B. oo   C. ew   D. ough

3. mild____
    A. o   B. oo   C. ew   D. ough

OTHER PATTERNS TO KEEP IN MIND

The Letters	Their Sounds	Examples
gh	f	cough
ch	k	stomach
ea	eh	bread

Practice 10: Other Patterns
6C1e, f, 6W2tech.d, 6W4c

Select the correct letters to fill in the blanks and make a complete word.

1. enou___
    A. ai   B. ea   C. ch   D. gh

2. a___e
    A. a   B. ea   C. ch   D. gh

3. dr___n
    A. ai   B. ea   C. ch   D. gh

MANY PEOPLE MISSPELL THESE WORDS

Even the best spellers miss a word here and there. Look at these words:

arctic, schedule, fascinate, personal, weird

To help you remember how to spell them, write them on a 3x5 card and study them.

Practice 11: Common Misspellings
6C1e, f, 6W2tech.d, 6W4c

Fill the blank with the word that is spelled correctly.

1. Jason called me on his _____ phone.

    A. celluler

    B. cellular

    C. celellur

    D. celuller

2. The group decided to go _____ at the lake.

    A. picnicng   B. picknicing   C. picnicking   D. picknicking

3. The student had an _____ with her teacher.

    A. argement   B. argument   C. argcument   D. arguament

4. Alyssa joined the rally _____.

    A. commite   B. comittee   C. committe   D. committee

5. The council has begun an _____ study of the problem.

    A. independant   B. independent   C. independint   D. independunt

6. Tod put the soft drinks into the _____.

    A. refrigerator   B. refrigerater   C. refridgerator   D. refridgerater

7. The math teacher gave two _____ in one week.

    A. quizs   B. quizzs   C. quizes   D. quizzes

8. He asked his sister to help him with his _____ lessons.

    A. grammer   B. grammir   C. grammar   D. grammor

9. The boys and girls were assigned to _____ busses.

    A. separete   B. seperate   C. sepirate   D. separate

10. Rafe took his cousin to play _____ golf.

    A. miniture   B. miniature   C. minieture   D. menieture

HOMONYMS

Homonyms are words that sound the same but are spelled differently.

Examples:

flower

flour

bare

bear

seam

seem

"...give me this day my daily prey, I pray..."

To spell homonyms correctly, you need to know their meanings. You can often tell the meaning of a word from its *context*, or placement in a sentence. The words around it will usually give you a clue to its meaning.

Example: He was awarded a _____ for his service to his country.

medal

meddle

The correct answer is *medal*.

Practice 12: Homonyms
6C1e, f, 6W2tech.d, 6W4c

Select the correct word in the following.

1. Put on a _____ of gloves.
   A. pear   B. pair   C. pare

2. I don't know what to _____ to the party.
   A. ware   B. wear   C. where

3. My backpack sometimes makes for a heavy _____ to carry around.
   A. lode   B. load   C. lowed

4. A _____ storm is coming; you can hear the thunder!
   A. rain   B. rein   C. reign

5. The _____ of flowers is lovely in the spring.
   A. sent   B. cent   C. scent

6. _____ all packed for the trip and are leaving today
   A. Their   B. There   C. They're

7. To "_____ the day" means to take advantage of every minute.
   A. seas   B. sees   C. seize

8. When we get to the corner, we have to turn _____.
   A. rite   B. right   C. write

9. The sun's _____ are warm on my shoulders.
   A. rays   B. raze   C. raise

10. She ate a _____ salad at lunch.
    A. caret   B. carat   C. carrot

11. I _____ to know why you said that.
    A. need   B. knead   C. kneed

12. His house is down that long _____.
    A. rode   B. road   C. rowed

REVISING AND PROOFREADING FOR SPELLING

Always check your written work for spelling errors. Consult the dictionary if you are not sure how to spell a word. If you are working on a computer, usually you can right-click on a word to check its spelling. But remember, computer spellcheckers won't catch homonym errors. Always be sure to read your work carefully.

Practice 13: Proofreading
6C1e, f, 6W2tech.d, 6W4c

Practice checking for spelling errors by completing the following.

Part I: Select the word that is NOT spelled correctly.

1. She was <u>awarded</u> a <u>bonus</u> and a <u>trophy</u> before <u>retireing.</u>

          A   **B**   **C**   **D**

2. The <u>soccer</u> team <u>rallyed</u> in the <u>final</u> minute of the <u>contest</u>.
           A   **B**   **C**   **D**

3. He <u>knew</u> that her <u>birthday</u> was <u>celebrated</u> on <u>Febuary</u> fourth.
         A   **B**   **C**   **D**

4. Her <u>uncle</u> was <u>employed</u> by the <u>Buraeu</u> of Land <u>Management.</u>
         A   **B**   **C**   **D**

Part II: Read the following passage, then answer the questions.

> **1** Every evening, thousands of bats fly over the lake looking for their dinner. **2** They send out a high-pitched squeak to locate insects for there meal. **3** The squeaks strike the insect and bounce back to the bat. **4** These reflected echoes can lead the bat to its dinner. **5** This very help-full hunting skill is called "echolocation." **6** The bat's enormous ears tell it weather the echoes are reflected by a tree or by its prey.

5. Which of these sentences contains a misused homonym word?
    A. sentence 1   B. sentence 2   C. sentence 3   D. sentence 4

6. How should sentence 5 be corrected?

    A. change *skill* to *skil*

    B. change *hunting* to *hunteng*

    C. change *helpfull* to *helpful*

    D. change *echolocation* to *echoelocation*

7. How should sentence 6 be corrected?

    A. change *prey* to *pray*

    B. change *echoes* to *echos*

    C. change *weather* to *whether*

    D. change *enormous* to *enormus*

Part III: Read the following passage, then answer the questions.

1 Harper decided to help his family conserve on the monthly heating bill. **2** It occured to him that cold air was seeping under the doorways each evening. **3** So he acquird some stretchable plastic tubes at the hardware emporium and filled them with sand. **4** Every night, he placed these tubes at the bottoms of each door. **5** As a result, cold drafts could not get in. **6** The following month, the family's heating bill went down by 17%.

8. How should sentence 2 be corrected?
    A. change *occured* to *occurred*
    B. change *seeping* to *seepeng*
    C. change *doorways* to *doorwayes*
    D. change *evening* to *eavning*

9. How should sentence 3 be corrected?
    A. change *filled* to *filed*
    B. change *plastic* to *plasstic*
    C. change *acquird* to *acquired*
    D. change *stretchable* to *stretchible*

10. How should sentence 4 be corrected?
    A. change *tubes* to *tubbes*
    B. change *door* to *dore*
    C. change *every* to *evry*
    D. change *bottems* to *bottoms*

CHAPTER 9 SUMMARY

Rules

Some rules are easier to remember than others. Keep in mind that there are **regular spellings** (which follow one set of rules) and **irregular spellings** (which follow different rules and have lots of exceptions). The *i before e* poem is an example of a simple rule to learn. Others, such as the rules for **plural formations of nouns and verbs**, will take time. But eventually, with practice, they will become second nature.

Sounds

As you read, notice the **different ways to spell** the same sounds. When you find one you don't recognize, put the word on a 3x5 card and study it when you have time.

With **homonyms**, the context around the word will usually tell you its meaning and lead you to its correct spelling.

CHAPTER 9 REVIEW

6C1e, f, 6W2tech.d, 6W4c

In the following sentences, choose the word that best fits in the blank.

1 Jeremy always _____ the four-o'clock bus.

   A taks   B takes   C taeks   D taiks

2 One of her favorite stories was "Snow White and the Seven _____."

   A Dwarefs   B Dwarvs   C Dwarfes   D Dwarves

Select the correct letters to fill in the blanks and make a complete word.

3 I counted twenty-____t birds perched in that tree.

   A ay   B ai   C ae   D eigh

4 Alth____. we had a big breakfast, we were hungry again by eleven.

   A o   B au   C oh   D ough

The following sentences contain errors in spelling. Select the word that is misspelled.

5 James is <u>trying</u> out for wide <u>reciever</u> on the <u>football</u> <u>squad</u>.
         A   B   C   D

6 Tomas <u>considered</u> winning the <u>spelling</u> bee his <u>greatest</u> <u>achievment.</u>
         A   B   C   D

7 The <u>students</u> felt a sense of <u>releif</u> when <u>their</u> exams were <u>completed</u>.
         A   B   C   D

Complete the following sentences with the correctly spelled words.

8 He_____ the two numbers and got the final answer.

   A multiplid   B multiplyd   C multiplyed   D multiplied

9 Club members _____ to change the meeting place.

   A agred   B agreed   C agrede   D agreede

10 Carly enjoyed _____ a few laps after practice.

   A runing   B running   C runneng   D runeing

11 Which word is spelled correctly?

A pageing   B bouncable   C changeable   D challengeing

12 Which word is NOT spelled correctly?

A doable   B bounced   C reversed   D guaranteing

Read the following sentence.

> The new equipment was enableing the workers to meet their goals.

13 What change, if any, should be made to the sentence?

A change *workers* to *workeres*   C change *equipment* to *equiptment*

B change *enableing* to *enabling*   D no change

Fill the blank with the word that is spelled correctly.

14 Rick always carried a lot of _____ change in his pockets.

A lose   B luze   C lusse   D loose

15 She gave me a _____ look.

A mischeifus   B mischiefous   C mischievous   D mischeivous

16 The student presented a _____ reading to the class.

A humaros   B humorus   C humarous   D humorous

Select the correct pair of words to fill the blanks in the following homonym definitions.

17 _____(something to carry water in)/ _____ (light in color)

A flue/flu   B urn/earn   C pail/pale

18 _____(part of a bicycle)/ _____ (to sell)

A tire/tyre   B wheel/wield   C pedal/peddle

Chapter 10
Purposes and Patterns for Writing

This chapter addresses the following GPS-based CRCT standards:

ELA6W1	The student produces writing that establishes an appropriate organizational structure, sets a context and engages the reader, maintains a coherent focus throughout, and provides a satisfying closure. The student
	a. Selects a focus, an organizational structure, and a point of view based on purpose, genre expectations, audience, length, and format requirements.
	c. Uses traditional structures for conveying information (e.g., chronological order, cause and effect, similarity and difference, and posing and answering a question).
	d. Uses appropriate structures to ensure coherence (e.g., transition elements).

WHY DO AUTHORS WRITE?

Authors write for many reasons. Authors may want to do the following:

- give you some information
- describe something for you
- persuade you to do something
- entertain you

It will help you to know some of the ways in which writers organize their work.

They may use any of these kinds of organization:

- chronological order
- cause and effect
- similarity and difference
- question and answer

When you write, *you* become an author.

CHOOSING A PATTERN FOR ORGANIZATION

To decide on which of these patterns to follow, ask yourself:

"What am I trying to do with this piece of writing?"

Let's say that you want to tell an entertaining story about a summer trip. You decide to tell the story's events in the order that they occurred. So you use…

CHRONOLOGICAL ORDER

To begin, you would do the following:

1. Write down the things that happened on the trip.

2. Put these events in order—give each a number: 1, 2, 3, etc.

3. Write an opening "topic" statement that shows readers what the story will be about.

> **Example:** "Several crazy things happened to me when I went to the lake last summer."

4. Write a draft describing each event as it happened.

5. Use *transitional* words and phrases to connect these events.

Practice 1:   Chronological Order
6W1a, c

Use the information about order to answer the following questions.

Here are some events that are out of order. Put them in the correct sequence.

> 1 pour the boiling water into the teacup
>
> 2 fill the teapot with water
>
> 3 wait until the water boils
>
> 4 place the teapot on the stove

1.   Select the correct sequence of events.
   A. 1-2-4-3   B. 2-4-3-1   C. 3-4-1-2   D. 4-2-1-3

> 1 light the charcoal
>
> 2 put the steaks onto the grill
>
> 3 place the charcoal into the grill
>
> 4 wait until the charcoal is red hot

2.   Select the correct sequence of events.
   A. 1-3-2-4   B. 2-3-4-1   C. 3-1-4-2   D. 4-3-1-2

Read this passage. Then answer the questions.

> **1** Chad assembled his fishing rod and attached a lure. **2** He waded out into a shallow part of the river. **3** Soon he felt a tug on the line, and he reeled it in. **4** He cast his line into the river and waited. **5** A wriggling rainbow trout was his prize.

3. Which sentence is out of order in this passage?
   A. sentence 2   B. sentence 3   C. sentence 4   D. sentence 5

Read this sentence:

> He admired the sleek fish and then allowed it to swim back to its home in the river.

4. Where would this sentence BEST fit into the passage above?
   A. after sentence 2   C. after sentence 4

   B. after sentence 3   D. after sentence 5

CHRONOLOGICAL ORDER TRANSITIONS

Writers use transitions to keep their ideas flowing smoothly. These words and phrases may tell readers that something new is coming. Or they may reveal a change in direction.

In chronological structure, transitions can show the time covered. They can indicate that something is being added to the story.

Time Order	Adding Facts
first, next, then, later, finally	and, too, further, in addition, after that

Practice 2: Chronological Order Transitions
6W1d

Use the information about transitions to answer the following questions.

Read this passage and answer the questions.

> **1** It was time to set up the tent. **2** We unrolled the ground sheet that goes under the tent. **3** We pegged the ground sheet down. **4** We put the tent poles through the loops. **5** We put the tent up and pulled out the guy lines. **6** We pegged the guy lines down, and the tent was set.

1. What is the BEST word to add before sentence 2?
   A. First   B. Next   C. Then   D. Later

2. What is the BEST word to add before sentence 3?
   A. First   B. Next   C. Later   D. Finally

3. What is the best word to add before sentence 6?
   A. Then   B. Later   C. Next   D. Finally

Read the first sentence of the next paragraph of the story.

> We were hot and sweaty, so we all ran down to the lake for a swim.

4. Which of the following is the BEST transition to begin the sentence?
   A. And   B. Further   C. After that   D. In addition

CAUSE AND EFFECT

Using a **cause and effect** pattern, a writer shows why things happen or shows the outcome of actions. The writer can start with a **cause** (why or how something happened) and then show **effects** (the results). There can be one cause or many causes. There can also be one effect or many effects.

In writing, this pattern can also be turned around.

> **Example:** In a detective story, an author often starts by showing an effect—the crime. The writer then explores how and why the crime happened—the cause.

Read these two news stories.

1. Cause-Effect Pattern

> A heavy thunderstorm hit the Atlanta area last night. As a result, trees and power lines were knocked down. Many Atlanta residents were left in the dark, without electric power. On the rain-slick highways, auto accidents were common.

2. Effect-Cause Pattern

> Atlanta residents were in the dark last night, without light or heat.
>
> The reason was a heavy thunderstorm that battered the area. Trees and power lines were down, and the accident rate soared on rain-slick highways.

Practice 3:   Cause and Effect
6W1a, c

Use the information about cause and effect patterns to answer the following questions.

Read the following sentences.

> Team members celebrated the victory by dumping a tub of Gatorade onto their coach.

1. Which of the following is the MOST likely cause of this effect?

    A. The football team began football practice yesterday.

    B. The football team will play its first game of the season tonight.

    C. The football team won the league championship today.

    D. The football team attended a team banquet last evening.

> A severe drought hit the area this year.

2. What is the MOST likely effect of this cause?
    A. Students attend a job fair.   C. The City Council passes a law.

    B. Farmers' incomes go down.   D. Local residents take vacations.

Read this passage. Answer the questions that follow.

1 Christopher Columbus discovered the New World by accident. **2** He was not trying to prove that the world was round. **3** In his time, people already knew that. **4** Columbus wanted to find an ocean route to the Indies. **5** He set sail using ancient maps and the night sky to find his way. **6** But his maps left out a large land mass that no Western Europeans knew about—North and South America. **7** Columbus stumbled onto our continent without meaning to. **8** And, of course, the land was already occupied—by Native Americans.

3. Which sentence states the main effect of Columbus's voyage?
   A. sentence 1   B. sentence 2   C. sentence 3   D. sentence 4

4. Which sentence states the main cause for Columbus discovering our continent?
   A. sentence 5   B. sentence 6   C. sentence 7   D. sentence 8

CAUSE AND EFFECT TRANSITIONS

When you use a cause and effect pattern, you will need certain words to link your ideas together. Transitions tell your reader that something is changing. They also work to link paragraphs together. Their purpose is to keep the writer's ideas flowing in good order.

Cause and Effect Transitions
because, for, since, as a result, due to, for the reason that, leads to, if...then, therefore, whereas

Practice 4: Cause and Effect Transitions
6W1d

Use the information about transitions to answer the following questions.

A special all-day conference of teachers will be held this Friday. There will be no classes on that day.

1. What is the BEST transition to place before the second sentence?
   A. Since   B. Due to   C. Because   D. Therefore

| If my sister can get the day off, _____ we will go surfing on Monday. |

2. What is the BEST transition to put in the blank?
   A. then
   B. leads to
   C. whereas
   D. for the reason that

Read the following passage, and then answer the questions.

1 Small insects have no hope of escaping the pitcher plant. **2** This plant has hollow, tube-like leaves that hold water. **3** These leaves produce a sweet odor that attracts bugs. **4** The plant's sticky hairs prevent the bug from crawling out. **5** It falls into the water and rots. **6** The pitcher plant digests the bug.

3. Which transition BEST fits before sentence 5?
   A. Since
   B. Because
   C. As a result
   D. For the reason that

4. Which transition BEST fits before sentence 6?
   A. Then
   B. Due to
   C. Because
   D. Leads to

5. Which of the following transitional phrases BEST fits before sentence 4?
   A. Once inside,
   B. In other words,
   C. As a result of,
   D. In the meantime,

SIMILARITY AND DIFFERENCE

In this method of organization, a writer makes a **comparison or contrast** of two different things. This can be a good form to use for a persuasive essay. One point of view can be compared to another to make a point. This pattern may also be called comparison and contrast.

Example: You decide to compare two speeches, one by Martin Luther King Jr. and the other by John F. Kennedy. You may find many similarities, or you might find interesting differences.

There are two basic forms for this pattern:

Block form: you describe one thing in detail and then go on to describe the thing that you are comparing it to. It would look like this in a diagram: AAA BBB.

Examples:

A In the old days, a golf ball was made of goose feathers stuffed into a leather cover. **A** It was relatively soft and could not be driven very far. **A** It also fell apart after a few rounds and had to be replaced.

B Today's golf ball has a dual core. **B** It is wrapped tightly in elastic. **B** It can be driven three hundred yards or more by a pro golfer. **B** And it will last until you lose it.

Point by point: each side of the issue is discussed in alternating style: A B A B A B

Example:

These two bugs are often confused. **A** The centipede is usually about one to two inches long. **B** The millipede can be as long as nine inches. **A** Centipedes eat other insects, while **B** millipedes feed only on plant life. **A** Centipedes are poisonous; **B** millipedes are not.

Practice 5: Similarity and Difference
6W1a, c

Use the information about similarity and difference to answer the following questions.

1 For many years, Pluto was thought to be a planet. **2** Today, astronomers call it a "dwarf planet." **3** Long ago, it was believed that Pluto was about the same size as the earth. **4** Scientists now know that it is much smaller—actually not as large as our moon. **5** Our planet has an atmosphere of breathable air. **6** Pluto is covered in frozen gases—methane, ammonia, and nitrogen. **7** Earth temperatures vary from hot to cold. **8** Pluto is permanently frozen at about minus 230 degrees.

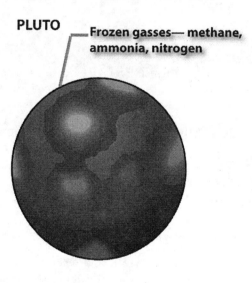

PLUTO

Frozen gasses— methane, ammonia, nitrogen

1. Which sentence contrasts with sentence 6?

    A. sentence 4   B. sentence 5   C. sentence 7   D. sentence 8

2. Which sentence contrasts with sentence 4?

    A. sentence 1   B. sentence 2   C. sentence 3   D. sentence 5

3. To change this passage from point by point to block form, which sentences should come first?

   A. 1-3-4-6   B. 1-3-6-8   C. 3-4-5-7   D. 3-5-6-8

4. A comparison-contrast pattern would work BEST for which of the following topics?

   A. the early life of Mark Twain

   B. the first science fiction novel

   C. Lewis Carroll's *Alice's Adventures in Wonderland*

   D. characters in *The Wizard of Oz* and a *Harry Potter* book

SIMILARITY AND DIFFERENCE TRANSITIONS

These transitions can be used within sentences or between sentences. They can also be used between paragraphs. They can also be used between paragraphs. They make the reader aware of the relationship between various aspects of two items being compared or contrasted.

Similarity and Difference Transitions	
Similarity (comparison)	**Difference (contrast)**
also, while, both, similarly, equally, in addition	although, even though, but, yet, however, on the other hand, on the other side

Practice 6: Similarity and Difference Transitions
6W1d

Look at the passage about Pluto, and then answer the questions.

1. Which transition would BEST go before sentence 5?

   A. Both   B. Equally   C. Even though   D. In addition

Read these sentences from the passage.

> **5** Our planet has an atmosphere of breathable air. **6** Pluto is covered in frozen gases – methane, ammonia and nitrogen.

2. What is the BEST way to combine these sentences?

   A. While our planet has an atmosphere of breathable air, Pluto is covered in frozen gases—methane, ammonia, and nitrogen.

   B. However, our planet has an atmosphere of breathable air, Pluto is covered in frozen gases—methane, ammonia, and nitrogen.

   C. Similarly, our planet has an atmosphere of breathable air, Pluto is covered in frozen gases—methane, ammonia, and nitrogen.

   D. Yet our planet has an atmosphere of breathable air, Pluto is covered in frozen gases—methane, ammonia, and nitrogen.

Read the following passage, and answer the questions.

> **1** A leaf blower works well in the fall. **2** Those dry leaves can be moved around easily with a jet of air. **3** You have a nice pile ready to bag and haul away. **4** After a steady rain, it's a different story. **5** You aim your leaf blower at those soggy leaves, and they won't budge. **6** It's time to get out the rake and shovel.

3.   What transition BEST fits before sentence 3?
     A. Yet   B. Both   C. Soon   D. While

4.   What transition BEST fits before sentence 4?
     A. But   B. Also   C. Equally   D. Although

5.   What transition BEST fits before sentence 5?
     A. However   C. Even though

     B. Similarly   D. On the other hand

POSING AND ANSWERING A QUESTION

There are two main reasons why a writer will use a **question and answer** organizational pattern:

1   Ask an interesting question and explore its answers.

Kiwi

> **Example:** Why are there birds that can't fly? Birds like the kiwi and the giant parrot have lost the ability to fly because there is plenty of food on the ground. In addition, they live on islands where there are no enemies hunting them.

2   Persuade readers to accept a certain point of view.

> **Example:** Should the government spend more money on education in the arts? I think it should since people have a need to express themselves through painting, music, theater, dance, poetry and other artistic forms. If a nation spends money just to educate engineers and scientists, it will be a very dull place.

The purpose of the question is to arouse reader interest. It should make the reader want to read more.

The body of a question-and-answer essay can follow any of these organizational structures:

- chronological
- cause and effect
- similarity and difference

Practice 7: Question and Answer
6W1a, c

Use the information about question and answer form to answer the following questions.

> **1** What color is light? **2** To find out, you first must get a flashlight and a prism. **3** Next, shine the light through the prism. **4** At this point, you will see a rainbow of colors. **5** Thus, you will realize that light is made up of many colors. **6** Isaac Newton first conducted this experiment many years ago.

1. Which words from the passage tell you that it follows a chronological pattern?
   - A. first, next, at this point
   - B. what, to find out, you will see
   - C. flashlight, prism, rainbow
   - D. shine the light, you will realize that

2. Which sentence answers the question?
   - A. sentence 3
   - B. sentence 4
   - C. sentence 5
   - D. sentence 6

3. What is the main purpose of this passage?
   - A. to inform
   - B. to question
   - C. to persuade
   - D. to entertain

Read this passage, and then answer the questions.

> **1** Why do they call it a computer "bug"? **2** The answer will surprise you. **3** Today, a bug is an error in the coding of a computer program. **4** But in 1945, when computers were first being developed, that word didn't apply. **5** One day, a woman named Grace Hopper was working on an early computer. **6** Suddenly the machine shut down, so the technicians opened it up to find out what was wrong. **7** They found a moth stuck inside a relay. **8** The bug was cutting off the flow of electricity. **9** The operators removed the moth and noted for the first time that a computer had been "debugged." **10** The term stuck.

4. Which sentence is designed to arouse reader interest?
   A. sentence 2   B. sentence 3   C. sentence 4   D. sentence 5

5. This passage combines two organizational patterns. What are they?
   A. question and answer plus effect-cause

   B. effect-cause plus compare-contrast

   C. cause-effect plus question and answer

   D. compare-contrast plus chronological

QUESTION AND ANSWER TRANSITIONS

Words that are used as connecters in a question and answer essay are the same as those used in the other organizational patterns.

Question and Answer Transitions
why, what, where, when, how, which
inversion of sentences into questions

Practice 8: Question and Answer Transitions
6W1d

Use the information about transitions to answer the following questions.

Read this passage, and answer the questions.

1 Should cough and cold medicines be given to children under six years of age? **2** Parents say that these medicines seem to relieve cold and flu symptoms. **3** A Federal Drug Authority group disagrees. **4** This group says that these medicines should not be given to young kids. **5** Parents respond that the medicines probably don't do any harm. **6** Doctors say that they are concerned about the side effects of these over-the-counter medications on children. **7** Children with allergies might benefit from certain medicines, though doctors issued a warning. **8** Pills taken for coughs and colds cause drowsiness and can be dangerous for kids.

9 Doctors note that these medicines are not even very effective for adults. **10** A study revealed that cough and cold medicines offered only a six percent improvement in the symptoms of adult users.

1. What MOST shows that this is written in a question and answer pattern?
   A. use of the transition *why*
        C. use of the transition *how*

   B. use of the transition *where*
        D. use of an inverted sentence

2. What transition BEST fits before sentence 3?
    A. However   B. Then   C. Also   D. As a result

3. What transition BEST fits before sentence 6?
    A. At this point   B. After that   C. Soon   D. But

4. What transition BEST fits before sentence 7?
    A. Next   C. Neither

    B. Even though   D. For the reason that

5. What transition BEST fits before sentence 9?
    A. Although   B. First   C. Since   D. In addition

CHAPTER 10 SUMMARY

There are four basic **organizational patterns** a writer can use to organize writing:

Chronological order tells a story the way it happened, in first-second-third order.

Cause and effect works in one of two ways:

- to describe a cause and then show its results
- to describe an effect and then show what caused it

Similarity and Difference compares or contrasts two different things. This pattern is also known as comparison and contrast.

Question and answer starts with a question and then answers it. The body of this type of essay can follow any one of the other organizational patterns.

Transition words are important in any organizational pattern. Transitions are like signs, pointing the way between ideas.

CHAPTER 10 REVIEW

6W1a, c, d

Check your knowledge by answering these questions:

1. **Which words indicate a chronological structure?**

   A in fact, evidently

   B following that, eventually

   C for example, to demonstrate

   D both of these, in the same way

2. **You want to write a story about a crime-solving detective. Which organizational pattern would BEST work for this kind of story?**

   A chronological

   B cause-effect

   C effect-cause

   D compare/contrast

Read this sentence.

> When will this city repair the ancient Fourth Street Bridge?

3. **This question is MOST likely the first sentence of an article designed to**

   A inform   B instruct   C entertain   D persuade

4. **What is the BEST way to change the question into a statement?**

   A The Fourth Street Bridge was constructed in 1957.

   B Heavy traffic jams the Fourth Street Bridge during rush hour.

   C It is time for the city to repair the ancient Fourth Street Bridge.

   D Bridge repair is the responsibility of the City Maintenance Department.

5. **You are writing a summary of a film that tells a fascinating story. Which organizational pattern will work BEST for your review?**

   A cause-effect

   B chronological

   C compare/contrast

   D question/answer

Look at this series of events:

1 pour chocolate syrup on top

2 scoop the ice cream out of the container

3 add whipped cream

4 place the ice cream into a bowl

6　**What is the correct sequence of events?**

A 1-4-3-2　　　　**B** 2-4-1-3　　　　**C** 3-1-4-2　　　　**D** 4-2-1-3

7　**Which word BEST fills the blank in this sentence?**

> We celebrated Greg's birthday with homemade pizza. _____, we all went to the roller rink.

A Further　　　　**B** Finally　　　　**C** After that　　　　**D** In addition

8　**You want to write a paper about the pyramids of Egypt. Which of the following would best compare/contrast with that topic?**

A the Eiffel Tower of Paris　　　　**C** the American Civil War

B the moon landing　　　　**D** the Internet

Read this sentence.

> The mountain gorilla is very dependent on the African forests that are its home, but the population of this animal is in danger of shrinking.

9　**What is the MOST likely cause of this effect?**

A People are changing forests into farmlands.

B The number of tourists to Africa has increased.

C Heavy rains have caused overgrowth in African forests.

D Scientists need to study rare animals in their home area.

10　**Which transitional words indicate a compare/contrast structure?**

A at this point, soon, now

B neither, equally, however

C due to, since, as a result

D then, for the reason that, later

Read this passage, then answer the questions.

> **1** Many animals feed on the leaves of trees. **2** Since trees grow new leaves every year, this feeding can strip a tree. **3** Grasses grow from the bottom up. **4** When animals eat the tips of grasses, the grass can continue growing.

11 Which sentences represent effects?

A sentences 1 and 3

B sentences 2 and 4

C sentences 2 and 3

D sentences 3 and 4

12 Which transition BEST fits before sentence 3?

A Since

B However

C In the meantime

D For the reason that

13 Which transition BEST fits before sentence 4?

A Then   B Finally   C Because   D Therefore

14 A compare/contrast organization would work BEST for which of the following topics?

A the origins of rap music

B the invention of the electric guitar

C the influence of the Beatles on American music

D the lives of musicians Duke Ellington and George Gershwin

15 Read this sentence. Then decide which transitional words BEST fit in the blanks.

_____ Alex had never lost a cross-country race, and _____ Richard had a sore ankle that day, Richard won the race by three yards.

A Even though/however

B Although/similarly

C Even though/even though

D While/therefore

Read these sentences from a report.

> It is a disgrace. We had to spend half a day just picking up trash and garbage around our campsite. The forest rangers said that there isn't much they can do about it.

16 What is the BEST question to introduce this report?

A How long can people camp in a state park?

B What are the duties of the forest rangers in our state park?

C Where is the best place in our state park to find a clean campsite?

D When are campers in the state park going to be forced to clean up their campsites?

> Teachers at your school are debating whether to lengthen the school year into the summer months. You decide to write a letter that presents what would be positive and negative about taking this step.

17 Which organizational pattern would work BEST for this letter?

A chronological

B cause-effect

C effect-cause

D compare/contrast

18 You are thinking of the best way to begin the letter. Which of the following would BEST catch reader attention?

A Let's make the school year longer, or not.

B This is a letter about the proposed expansion of the school year.

C Are there some good reasons to extend the school year?

D We don't want to do homework year-round, but teachers know we can learn more.

Chapter 11
Working with Paragraphs

This chapter addresses the following GPS-based CRCT standards:

ELA6W2	The student demonstrates competence in a variety of genres.
	The student produces a **narrative** (fictional, personal) that:
	b. Creates an organizing structure appropriate to the purpose, audience, and context.
	e. Excludes extraneous details and inconsistencies.
	f. Provides a sense of closure appropriate to the writing.
	The student produces writing (multi-paragraph **expository** composition such as description, explanation, comparison and contrast, or problem and solution) that:
	b. Establishes a statement as the main idea or topic sentence.
	c. Develops a controlling idea that conveys a perspective on the subject
	d. Creates an organizing structure appropriate to purpose, audience, and context.
	e. Develops the topic with supporting details.
	f. Excludes extraneous and inappropriate information.
	g. Follows an organized pattern appropriate to the type of composition.
	h. Concludes with a detailed summary linked to the purpose of the composition.
	The student produces **technical** writing (friendly letters, thank-you notes, formula poems, instructions) that:
	a. Creates or follows an organizing structure appropriate to the purpose, audience, and context.
	b. Excludes extraneous and inappropriate information
	c. Follows an organizational pattern appropriate to the type of composition.
ELA6W4	The student consistently uses the writing process to develop, revise, and evaluate writing. The student
	b. Revises manuscripts to improve the organization and consistency of ideas within and between paragraphs

In chapter 10, you took a look at some basics about writing. You learned that writing has many purposes. You also learned that organization is an important part of good writing.

In this chapter, you will learn more about paragraphs. Paragraphs are the building blocks for longer writing. A good paragraph must have a clear controlling idea (main idea). There must also be strong details that support that idea. Finally, there must be a strong conclusion.

Let's begin by looking at what it means to develop a controlling idea.

DEVELOPING A CONTROLLING IDEA

The first key to writing a good paragraph is creating a **controlling idea**. The controlling idea is the focus of the paragraph. It is the main idea. Without a clear controlling idea, a paragraph can confuse a reader.

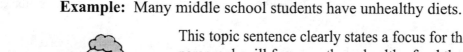

CREATING A TOPIC SENTENCE

A writer uses a **topic sentence** to present a controlling idea. A good topic sentence is easy for the reader to understand. It also makes the controlling idea easy to identify. A topic sentence can be located at the beginning or in the middle of a paragraph. It can even be located at the end.

> **Example:** Many middle school students have unhealthy diets.

This topic sentence clearly states a focus for the reader. This paragraph will focus on the unhealthy food that middle school students eat. The writer may give some specific examples of foods that should not be eaten.

> **Example:** There are several qualities that one should look for in a good friend.

This topic sentence presents this controlling idea—the qualities that make a good friend. A reader could expect to read about character traits and behaviors to look for in a friend.

Practice 1: Controlling Ideas and Topic Sentences
6W2exp.b

Use the paragraph below to answer this question.

1 What happens when you hear those words, "We are now going to split up into study groups"? **2** Some students cheer, and others groan. **3** Study groups have both positive and negative possibilities. **4** It's great to be able to work with your friends, but it is so easy to get distracted. **5** Sometimes peers give great input for the task at hand. **6** Other times, working with peers is like working with a bump on a log.

1. Which sentence is the topic sentence of the above paragraph?

   A. sentence 1   B. sentence 2   C. sentence 3   D. sentence 4

Use the paragraph below to answer this question.

1 The "tween" years are a time for discovery. **2** In fact, middle school is a great time to try different extracurricular pursuits. **3** Most middle schools offer sports, such as basketball, volleyball, and soccer. **4** Many middle schools also have clubs, such as Jr. Beta and Literary Magazine. **5** Some middle schools even have special groups for kids who are interested in anime, world cultures, and French cooking. **6** With all of these options, trying out activities should be an adventure.

2. Which sentence is the topic sentence of the above paragraph?

   A. sentence 1   B. sentence 2   C. sentence 3   D. sentence 4

Use the paragraph below to answer this question.

1 It had been about three hours since Toni returned home from summer camp. **2** As she looked lazily out the bedroom window, her mind began to wander. **3** Toni's mind drifted to thoughts about all of the fun she had enjoyed with new friends at Camp Kirklake. **4** There were early morning mountain hikes, potato sack races, and scavenger hunts. **5** At night, they would sit around the fire, making s'mores and talking about everything from Bigfoot to lip gloss. **6** What a great time it had been.

3. Which sentence is the topic sentence of the above paragraph?

   A. sentence 1   B. sentence 2   C. sentence 3   D. sentence 4

Use the paragraph below to answer this question.

Summer vacation is here, and it's time to get a job. If you are not sure what you want to do with your time off, you should know that teens have many options for summer jobs. Many companies hire fourteen-year-olds. You could bag groceries or work for an amusement park. You could even volunteer your time at a hospital and gain great experience for the future. Whether you decide on a paying or non-paying job, there's plenty out there for a teen to do during the summer.

4. What is the main idea of this paragraph?

   A. Teens should start working when they turn fourteen.

   B. Teens can work during the summer or after school during the school year.

   C. Teens can work in many different places during the summer.

   D. Non-paying jobs can be just as beneficial as those that pay.

Use the paragraph below to answer this question.

Daily exercise can be a drag. From day to day, there are so many tasks to complete. When can you find the time for exercise? Of course, research shows that exercise is important to a healthy life. People who get regular exercise avoid many illnesses. In addition, exercise reduces stress. Finding time for daily exercise might be difficult, but it is certainly worthwhile in the long run.

5. What is the main idea of this paragraph?

   A. It is difficult to find time for exercise.

   B. People who exercise will live longer.

   C. It is worthwhile to find time for exercise.

   D. Exercising must be enjoyable.

SUPPORTING DETAILS

A good paragraph begins with a topic sentence that states the controlling idea. A writer must also give strong support to the focus of the paragraph. To do this, a writer uses ideas that help to prove the main idea of the paragraph. These ideas are called **supporting details**.

WHICH SUPPORTING DETAILS ARE IMPORTANT?

Good supporting details reinforce the controlling idea of the paragraph. This makes good writing coherent, or easy to understand. Also, good writing will have unity. This means that all supporting details relate to the controlling idea. Let's take a look at an example.

There are so many great desserts that are fun to enjoy during the summer. One kind of dessert, cold desserts, includes everything from cold cakes and pies to ice cream in its many versions. Summer music is great to enjoy with ice cream. Some people enjoy cheesecakes with fresh summer fruit. Others might opt for a banana split heaped with toppings. Whatever the choice, there is nothing more relaxing than sweet fun in the sun!

In this paragraph, one sentence is clearly out of place. Since the paragraph is about summer desserts, the writer disrupts unity with this sentence:

Summer music is great to enjoy with ice cream.

While this may be a true statement, it has nothing to do with the paragraph focus—summer desserts. That sentence does not relate to the main idea.

In some cases, writers restate some details that have already been discussed in an earlier part of the paragraph. Let's take a look at an example.

Parents can teach teens long-lasting values. There are many ways that teens can begin to establish good values. Many options are available to parents who want to instill values in their teens. For example, it is a good idea for parents to require their teens to do chores in exchange for privileges. This teaches teens that they must earn the things they value. Teens can also take care of pets. This teaches teens to be unselfish and to regard the lives of others. If parents want to raise responsible adults, they should start by making responsible teenagers.

The third sentence contains a detail that does not need to be repeated. It uses different words to restate the same idea found in the second sentence. Writers should avoid repeating details if it is not necessary.

Practice 2:   Supporting Details
6W2nar.e, exp.e, f, tech.b

Use the paragraph below to answer this question.

1 A balanced life includes several factors. **2** Family and friends help to make life enjoyable. **3** Going out for ice cream with friends is fun. **4** Time should be given to personal interests, reading, or sports. **5** Staying focused in school is also an important part of a full and healthy life.

1. Which sentence does not relate to the rest of the paragraph above and should be removed?

    A. sentence 2   B. sentence 3   C. sentence 4   D. sentence 5

Use the paragraph below to answer this question.

1 Hard work in school pays off for students. **2** Students who work hard by doing their best and maintaining good study habits are appreciated by parents and teachers. **3** These students earn a sense of accomplishment for themselves. **4** It is great to have a game day at school. **5** Most importantly, when students work hard, they have more opportunities for the future.

2. Which sentence does not relate to the rest of the paragraph above and should be removed?

    A. sentence 1   B. sentence 2   C. sentence 3   D. sentence 4

Use the paragraph below to answer this question.

1 There are many qualities that go into the making of a good book. **2** For one, good books have strong plots. **3** They are full of adventure or interesting drama that keeps the reader turning page after page. **4** Many teen readers like fantasy novels set in the future. **5** Good books also have interesting characters. **6** These people often seem real to the reader. **7** Lastly, suspense is often a part of good books. **8** The anticipation of what will happen next is often enough to keep a reader wanting more. **9** Strong plots, characters, and suspense are a part of the great book formula.

3. Which sentence does not relate to the rest of the paragraph above and should be removed?

   A. sentence 2   B. sentence 3   C. sentence 4   D. sentence 5

Use the paragraph below to answer this question.

> **1** Dreams often do come true. **2** Some people have no dreams. **3** Teachers once dreamed of having their own classrooms. **4** Police officers dreamed of catching bad guys. **5** And animal doctors dreamed of helping cats and dogs. **6** Dreamers of today can become the success stories of tomorrow.

4. Which sentence does not relate to the rest of the paragraph above and should be removed?

   A. sentence 1   B. sentence 2   C. sentence 3   D. sentence 4

Use the paragraph below to answer this question.

> **1** Taking tests is an important part of student life. **2** Students must take tests to show that they understand what has been taught. **3** Sometimes tests are long and boring. **4** There are many types of tests that are given during a single school year. **5** Some standardized tests are given in the spring. **6** Most teachers give regular unit tests throughout the school year. **7** Tests give teachers valuable information about what students know.

5. Which sentence does not relate to the rest of the paragraph above and should be removed?

   A. sentence 1   B. sentence 2   C. sentence 3   D. sentence 4

Use the paragraph below to answer this question.

> **1** Middle schools often offer students extracurricular activities. **2** Some have athletic teams that practice when school gets out. **3** Beta club is another group that meets after school. **4** And once classes are dismissed, the Spanish club offers students the opportunity to learn about other cultures. **5** There is a place for everyone.

6. Which idea about extracurricular activities is stated too often?

    A. They are offered by most middle schools.

    B. They take place after regular classes.

    C. They include basketball and football.

    D. They sometimes require good grades.

Use the paragraph below to answer this question.

1 Students should treat substitute teachers with the same respect they give to their classroom teachers. **2** They should not behave in a different way than they do when the classroom teacher is in charge. **3** For example, students should still raise their hands to ask questions. **4** They should still sit in their assigned seats. **5** In general, how they behave for a substitute should be just as good as when the regular teacher is in charge.

7. Which idea about respecting substitute teachers is stated too often?

    A. There are often too many substitutes in a school.

    B. Students should respect substitutes.

    C. Student behavior for a substitute should be the same behavior that is appropriate for the regular teacher.

    D. Students should raise their hands and sit in their assigned seats even when there is a substitute in charge.

Use the paragraph below to answer this question.

1 Many parents do their best to help their children be successful. **2** Parents monitor their kids' grades. **3** They keep in touch with teachers. **4** Many parents do all that they can to ensure the success of their kids. **5** Parents also help children pursue personal interests. **6** They carpool them to sports. **7** They even help kids develop talents in music and dance. **8** Without parental support, many children would not be successful.

8. Which idea about parents helping with their children's success is stated too often?

   A. Parents do their best for the success of their children.

   B. Parents spend time carpooling.

   C. Children would be unsuccessful without supportive parents.

   D. Parents spend money on their children's interests.

ORGANIZING IDEAS

Good **organization** is important for clear paragraphs. If writing is not well organized, a reader can be confused. There are many ways to organize ideas. Three common **organizational patterns** are chronological order, spatial order, and order of importance. Let's look at each of these.

CHRONOLOGICAL ORDER

One pattern is **chronological order**. This means that details are arranged in time order. This pattern is useful when a writer is telling a story. Take a look at the following paragraph about a busy Saturday. This paragraph is a narrative paragraph; it tells a story. Notice how the events are written in time order.

Last Saturday was a very busy day. It started with a trip to the vet for Missy, our cocker spaniel. While at the vet's office, we had to break up a barking match between Missy and a feisty poodle. Then, Missy was so angry with the vet that we had to reschedule her for another Saturday appointment next week. Next, it was off to the mall for shoe shopping. There seemed to be a huge sale at almost every store. Lines stretched out into the mall. What should have taken no more than a half hour turned out to last all afternoon. Finally, it was back home for dinner. We arrived home to find that the refrigerator had gone out. What should have been our dinner was now unfit to eat. We collapsed onto the couch, tired from the day and waiting for pizza delivery. It was a day that I won't soon forget.

When you read this paragraph, you should have noticed how the writer retold the events in time order. Without this use of chronological order, this story would have been very difficult to understand.

SPATIAL ORDER

Another pattern for organizing ideas is to use **spatial order**. This means to organize details according to location. For example, a writer might write about details from top to bottom or right to left. This works best when writing paragraphs that use description. Take a look at the following paragraph that describes the layout of a classroom.

> Ms. Briggs's language arts classroom is neat, organized, and nicely arranged. As you enter the classroom, on the left is the student center. There, students find supplies and details on missed assignments. Straight ahead is Ms. Briggs's desk. It is neat and looks like a great place to get work done. She has a cup of red pens and a healthy green plant. Near the back of the room, there is a window that opens to the courtyard. There is also a bright red bulletin board. Ms. Briggs has the board decorated with pictures of her students and their favorite books. On the right side of the classroom is the resource wall. Ms. Briggs uses this wall to display language arts charts and definitions to help her students in class. Finally, Ms. Briggs's white board always neatly shows what students are to do for the day. Ms. Briggs has a model classroom.

The writer organized details about Ms. Briggs's classroom according to their arrangement. The writer does not jump around from place to place in the classroom. This would have been confusing for the reader. This is an example of how spatial order can be used to organize ideas.

ORDER OF IMPORTANCE

Arranging ideas in their **order of importance** is a third pattern that writers use to organize details. A writer might organize ideas from the least to the most important or the other way around. Take a look at a paragraph about youth responsibility. This paragraph uses order of importance.

Kids today have many responsibilities to consider. Most importantly, they must consider responsibilities about home and family. These may include spending family time and helping with household chores. They also have academic responsibility. During school, kids have the task of paying attention and doing their best to be successful. After school, they have homework, projects, and tests to which they must give personal time. Lastly, they have personal responsibilities to friends and personal hobbies. Some kids belong to gymnastic or karate leagues. Others like to spend time with friends from school, the neighborhood, or elsewhere. Any way you look at it, kids have plenty of ways to divide their time in a day.

In this paragraph, the writer arranged details from the most important to the least important. This clear pattern makes meaning easier for the reader.

ACHIEVING CLARITY THROUGH ORGANIZATION OF IDEAS

Regardless of the organizational pattern chosen by the writer, clarity is important. Without the proper organization of ideas, a writer will not be able to present ideas clearly to the reader. Let's take a look at an example of some sentences that need to be organized for the sake of clarity.

1. She would spend hours in the kitchen helping Grandma bake and prepare Sunday dinners.

2. Ever since she was a little girl, Erin has known that she wanted to be a chef. Her training began early.

3. Today, Erin is a top chef in an exclusive Manhattan eatery.

4. When she cooked on her own, Erin would even create her own versions of Easy Bake Oven recipes.

5. There, Erin learned cooking rules and technique that she still uses today.

Now, take a minute to look at the sentences and decide on the most effective way to order them. You should have ordered them this way: 2, 1, 5, 4, 3. Take a look at the most effective organization of this paragraph:

> Ever since she was a little girl, Erin has known that she wanted to be a chef. Her training began early. She would spend hours in the kitchen helping Grandma bake and prepare Sunday dinners. There, Erin learned rules and techniques that she still uses today. When she cooked on her own, Erin would even create her own versions of Easy Bake Oven recipes. Today, Erin is a top chef in an exclusive Manhattan eatery.

Practice 3: Organizing Ideas
6W2nar.b, exp.d, g, tech.a, c, 6W4B

Read each question, and choose the BEST answer.

1. Why do writers use organization and organizational patterns in paragraph writing?

    A. This gives clarity to the writing.

    B. The paragraph looks more attractive to the reader.

    C. The paragraph is then shorter.

    D. Most writers like to be organized.

2. Which organizational pattern uses time order?

    A. chronological

    B. spatial

    C. order of importance

3. Which organizational pattern might arrange description details from tallest to shortest or left to right?

    A. chronological

    B. spatial

    C. order of importance

Use the paragraph below to answer this question.

> **1** Ben woke up late for school and frantically jumped into the shower. **2** He threw on some clothes and didn't even think about fixing his hair. **3** It was Saturday! **4** As he rushed out the door he looked at his watch. **5** He knew that he was going to miss the bus. **6** Then he realized something even worse.

4. In the paragraph above, sentence 3 is out of order. Where should it BEST be placed?

    A. before sentence 1

    B. after sentence 1

    C. after sentence 5

    D. after sentence 6

Use the paragraph below to answer this question.

1 Leah had looked every-where, but there was no sign of her pink scarf. 2 What else could she wear to Stephanie's ice skating party? 3 Just then, it hit her. 4 The canary yellow scarf that her Nana had knitted for her last year would not coordinate with her frosted pink gloves and hat; only the pink scarf would work. 5 Leah ran to the puppy's play pen. 6 There it was! 7 Her schnauzer puppy, Chip, was all snuggled up in her pretty pink scarf. 8 With a sigh of relief and a smile, Leah decided that she could wait until after nap-time to retrieve the scarf.

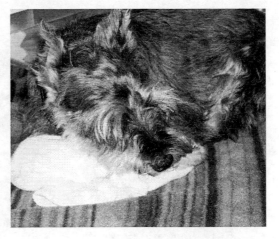

5. In the paragraph above, sentence 3 is out of order. Where should it BEST be placed?
   A. before sentence 1
   B. after sentence 2
   C. before sentence 4
   D. after sentence 4

Use the paragraph below to answer this question.

1 Min Sue stepped up to the stage with her lines in her hands and big dreams in her heart. 2 She had always known that she wanted to be on the big screen, and now was her chance. 3 As she stood in line wait-ing for a chance to read lines for the casting director, all Min Sue could think of was landing a spot on that cereal commercial. 4 Before long, the voice of a stage hand told her that she was up next. 5 This was her big chance to shine.

6. In the paragraph above, sentence 1 is out of order. Where should it BEST be placed?
   A. before sentence 1
   B. after sentence 2
   C. before sentence 4
   D. after sentence 5

Use the paragraph below to answer the question.

1 Manuel couldn't wait for three o'clock to come. 2 All day, he had been thinking about his birthday party after school, and now he was less than an hour away. 3 Resting his head on his folded arms, he settled in to the voice of Mrs. Sedowski's plant life lecture. 4 Hopefully, he could make it through this last hour of the school day. 5 Time dragged by in slow motion.

7. In the paragraph above, sentence 5 is out of order. Where should it BEST be placed?

   A. before sentence 1   C. after sentence 2

   B. after sentence 1   D. after sentence 3

Use the paragraph below to answer the question.

1 The zoo is a good place to take a warm weather trip. 2 It provides valuable science lessons, and it's a great place for a picnic lunch. 3 There are many options for school field trips throughout the year. 4 When the weather is cool, indoor places such as museums or planetariums make great trips. 5 In the fall, a corn maze/pumpkin patch adventure is a good way to enjoy seasonal sights. 6 In the winter, the Ice Capades are enjoyable. 7 With so many great options, teachers can plan exciting outings for students year round.

8. In the paragraph above, sentence 3 is out of order. Where should it BEST be placed?

   A. before sentence 1

   B. after sentence 3

   C. before sentence 5

   D. after sentence 5

WRAPPING IT UP

The **conclusion** is the final piece of paragraph writing. To conclude a paragraph well, a writer creates a strong closing sentence.

CREATING A CLOSING SENTENCE

A strong **closing sentence** must relate to the controlling idea of the paragraph. It should also offer a summary of the key points of the paragraph. Let's take a look at some examples.

Charlie has written a paragraph about the pros and cons of taking piano lessons. He is looking for a sentence to conclude his paragraph. Let's take a look at his paragraph and determine which choice would work best for him.

When it comes to taking piano lessons, there are both pros and cons to consider. One pro is that by taking these lessons, you may develop or improve your musical talent. This may help you in the future to earn honors or money. On the other hand, taking piano lessons may lessen the time you have with friends. While you are studying piano, your friends may be enjoying some new adventure without you.

Choice 1 These are the horrors of taking piano lessons.

Choice 2 These are the marvels of taking piano lessons.

Choice 3 In the end, you will have to decide if the pros of taking lessons outweigh the cons.

Choices 1 and 2 do not work. Charlie's paragraph is about the pros and cons of taking piano lessons. Both choice 1 and choice 2 focus only on one side. Choice 3, however, would conclude with the most balance. This option would work the best. Let's take a look at another example.

Damien has written a paragraph about the importance of playing school sports. He is looking for a sentence to conclude his paragraph. Which choice would work best for Damien's conclusion?

It is important for students to be able to play school sports. For one, playing sports helps students to focus on school work. Athletic teams often require a minimum GPA. This means that students often work hard in school to make sure that they will be able to participate. Also, playing school sports boosts self-esteem among students. As members of a team, students feel valued. They are proud of themselves for being able to contribute to a group of their peers. Last, playing school sports promotes a balanced lifestyle. It fulfills the need to exert physical energy while giving students an outlet to relieve stress.

Choice 1 Ultimately, playing school sports helps students to maintain good grades, self-confidence, and a healthy life.

Choice 2 Ultimately, students have so many opportunities to play school sports.

Choice 3 Ultimately, without playing school sports, students will not be successful.

Choice 1 seems to summarize three clear points that may have been a part of Damien's supporting details. Choice 2 makes a good point. However, it does not seem to belong at the end of this paragraph. It is not conclusive. Choice 3 is a strong opinion. Damien would have to follow it up with some details for support. It would not make a good conclusion. It seems that choice 1 is the best choice.

Practice 4: Writing Closing Sentences
6W2nar.f, exp.h, 6W4B

1. Which sentence would be the BEST closing sentence in the paragraph below?

> The debate over school uniforms is almost as old as the debate, "Which came first, the chicken or the egg." Those in favor say that uniforms reduce barriers between students. Those against say uniforms violate students' rights to express themselves. Some say school uniforms improve attendance. Others say uniforms are a financial burden to parents.

A. Many students want to wear what they choose.

B. Uniforms take away student choice.

C. There are many differing ideas about school uniforms.

D. Students should be allowed to make the final decision.

2. Which sentence would be the BEST closing sentence in the paragraph below?

Often, middle schoolers spend too much time watching TV. After school, many plop themselves in front of "the dummy box." They spend hours watching programs that have little educational value. Perhaps they could use this time better by studying or being with family. Middle school students who watch too much TV are losing out on valuable life experiences.

A. Watching too much TV can cost more than just wasted hours.

B. It would really help if parents monitored teen TV time.

C. Most young people who watch TV excessively will do so as adults.

D. Watching TV is dangerous and destructive.

3. Which sentence would be the BEST closing sentence in the paragraph below?

After a busy school year, some students break their routine and head to some type of summer camp. Summer camp offers a chance for students to break away from the daily grind. Most students attend camps that have some sort of focus. Sports, religion, and fine arts based camps are some specific examples. Students usually learn a great deal at camp while having fun and enjoying new experiences.

A. Summer camp is a way to break the routine after school ends.

B. Summer camps are boring and take kids away from neighborhood friends.

C. There are many types of summer camps from which to choose.

D. Some summer camps are in the mountains.

4. Which sentence would be the BEST closing sentence in the paragraph below?

Candice could not think of a thing to buy. What do you get a girl who already has it all? She and Kennedy had been friends since the first grade, but when it came to buying gifts for her best friend, Candice drew a blank. Suddenly it hit her—a box full of jelly beans! No one would think of that, and Kennedy would love it.

A. Jellybeans were very popular in their group of friends.

B. Now, Candice could get to the party.

C. Candice sighed with relief, heading for the candy store.

D. Kennedy was the best friend on earth.

5. Which sentence would be the BEST closing sentence in the paragraph below?

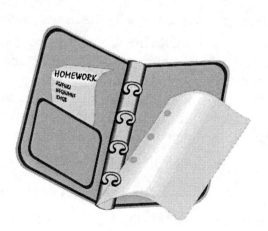

By the time they reach middle school, most students are ready to take on some responsibility. One task that middle schoolers should manage is homework assignments. Most schools issue planners to students to help them keep track of what is due when. Students can use these planners to record daily homework and make notes about tests and projects.

A. Planners are also a great place to jot down friends' cell phone numbers and e-mail addresses.

B. Planners are also used as hall passes.

C. Some student planners are very plain, while others have attractive designs.

D. Planners are a good starting place for middle schoolers to learn responsible habits.

CHAPTER 11 SUMMARY

The **controlling idea** is the focus or main idea of the paragraph.

The **topic sentence** states the controlling idea in a paragraph. A good topic sentence is clear, and it helps the reader to identify the paragraph's focus.

DON'T FORGET!

Supporting details help to prove the controlling idea. Good supporting details must reinforce the paragraph's focus.

Three commonly used **organizational patterns** are **chronological order**, **spatial order**, and **order of importance**.

Chronological order arranges ideas in time order.

Spatial order organizes details according to location.

In **order of importance**, a writer might organize ideas from the least to the most important or the other way around.

A strong **closing sentence** must relate to the controlling idea of the paragraph. It should also offer a good summary of the key points from the paragraph.

CHAPTER 11 REVIEW
6W2, 6W4b

For items, 1–5, read the paragraph provided. Then decide which sentence in the paragraph acts as the topic sentence.

Use the paragraph below to answer the question.

1 Friends make life better. **2** They share your jokes and fun. **3** They are also there when you need a shoulder for crying or an ear for listening. **4** Friends are there to talk to about anything under the sun. **5** Without friends, life wouldn't be as wonderful.

1   Which sentence is the topic sentence of the above paragraph?

   A sentence 1   **B** sentence 2   **C** sentence 3   **D** sentence 4

Use the paragraph below to answer the question.

1 Dionne stared at the blank paper. **2** She always had trouble with writing. **3** It was hard for her to know where to start. **4** She could never think of the words that would express exactly what she was thinking. **5** Writing always took her forever, and when she was finished, her work wasn't that great. **6** Yet, she stared at the paper, drawing a blank, hoping that help would come from somewhere.

2   Which sentence is the topic sentence of the above paragraph?

   A sentence 1   **B** sentence 2   **C** sentence 3   **D** sentence 4

Use the paragraph below to answer the question.

1 The librarian looked around her, wondering where to start. **2** There were two carts of unshelved books. **3** In the corner, where a group of students had been working last period, there was a collection of assorted candy wrappers. **4** The turn-in box was almost overflowing with books to be checked in and sorted. **5** Her desk in-box really was overflowing with unopened mail. **6** This afternoon was sure to be busy.

3   Which sentence is the topic sentence of the above paragraph?

   A sentence 2   **B** sentence 3   **C** sentence 5   **D** sentence 6

Use the paragraph below to answer the question.

> **1** When is a good time to start thinking about careers? **2** Some people believe that one cannot consider careers until high school or college. **3** However, adolescents begin to learn their strengths and weakness and likes and dislikes. **4** Just knowing these qualities makes early career decisions possible. **5** Middle school years are a great time for students to begin having some career ideas.

4 **Which sentence is the topic sentence of the above paragraph?**

   A sentence 1   **B** sentence 2   **C** sentence 4   **D** sentence 5

Use the paragraph below to answer the question.

> Swimming is a great total-body workout. It involves both the upper and lower body. Swimming helps build strength. It is also good for coordination. Anyone interested in a healthy way to keep the whole body toned should think about swimming.

5 **Which sentence is the topic sentence of the above paragraph?**

   A sentence 1   **B** sentence 2   **C** sentence 3   **D** sentence 4

For items 6–10, read each paragraph. Then decide which sentence in the paragraph does not relate to the rest of the paragraph and should be removed.

Use the paragraph below to answer the question.

> **1** Jessica was feeling nervous. **2** She had studied all week, gotten a good night's sleep, and eaten a balanced breakfast. **3** Yet now she sat waiting for the bell for second period, and all she could think was that she wasn't ready for her math test. **4** Fortunately, she was dressed nicely, so she didn't have to worry about that. **5** Trying to calm down, she pulled out a few flash cards and began going over formulas. **6** She hoped she would do well on the test.

6 **Which sentence does not relate to the rest of the paragraph above and should be removed?**

   A sentence 2   **B** sentence 3   **C** sentence 4   **D** sentence 5

Use the paragraph below to answer the question.

1 Mr. Russell looked at his students with pride. 2 Staring back, they couldn't figure out if his smile meant that they had done well on this week's vocabulary quiz or if he was simply having a good day. 3 Rico slammed his binder to the floor. 4 "Everyone made an *A*!" he said, to the cheers of the sixth grade classroom. 5 That afternoon, they celebrated with ice cream.

7 Which sentence does not relate to the rest of the paragraph above and should be removed?

   A sentence 1   **B** sentence 2   **C** sentence 3   **D** sentence 4

Use the paragraph below to answer the question.

1 It is fun to have a sleepover with friends. 2 To have the best sleepover, a few things must be available. 3 For one, there must be friends who love to laugh. 4 Also, there must be good junk food. 5 Some food favorites are pizza, hot dogs, and potato chips. 6 For entertainment, there must be games and movies. 7 Because of the frenzied atmosphere, dogs sometimes cause trouble at sleepovers. 8 Last, there must be a responsible parent to chaperone.

8 Which sentence does not relate to the rest of the paragraph above and should be removed?

   A sentence 2   **B** sentence 5   **C** sentence 6   **D** sentence 7

Use the paragraph below to answer the question.

1 Social studies can be very interesting. 2 During social studies, students learn about state, national, and world events. 3 Jeremy usually sleeps right through class. 4 By studying history, students learn to understand the world. 5 Social studies is both important and fun to learn.

9 Which sentence does not relate to the rest of the paragraph above and should be removed?

   A sentence 1   **B** sentence 2   **C** sentence 3   **D** sentence 4

Use the paragraph below to answer the question.

> **1** Manuel had jogged to school that day. **2** There was no way he was going to be unprepared for his noon race with Justin. **3** He wondered if Justin would show up. **4** He had trained all week, running around the block until the street lights came on. **5** He knew that he was the faster kid; he just had to run his best race.

10 Which sentence does not relate to the rest of the paragraph above and should be removed?

A sentence 1   **B** sentence 2   **C** sentence 3   **D** sentence 4

For 11–15, read each paragraph. Then, decide where the sentence that is out of order should be placed.

Use the paragraph below to answer the question.

> **1** Spread the jelly on one slice. **2** To make a super PBJ sandwich, start with two slices of bread. **3** Spread the peanut butter on the other slice. **4** Put the two sides together, with peanut butter facing jelly. **5** Enjoy!

11 In the paragraph above, sentence 1 is out of order. Where should it BEST be placed?

A after sentence 2   **C** after sentence 4

B before sentence 4   **D** after sentence 5

Use the paragraph below to answer the question.

> **1** Just then, she heard the noise of a gruff old dog bark from behind. **2** Glancing over her shoulder, Cherelle thought she was in the clear. **3** She could no longer hear Mr. Miller's mean dog, Squatty, running behind her. **4** Now, she could pedal a bit slower. **5** Hurried canine footsteps were gaining on her. **6** Oh no!

12 In the paragraph above, sentence 1 is out of order. Where should it BEST be placed?

A after sentence 2   **C** after sentence 4

B after sentence 3   **D** after sentence 5

Use the paragraph below to answer the question.

1 The artist stood back to admire her work. **2** For a moment, the artist looked down to pick up her charcoal to make one final touch. **3** This was the best caricature she had done today. **4** She had captured the shy but good-natured personality of her model. **5** The features she had sketched were as clearly recognizable as those of the woman that posed before her easel. **6** When she looked back up toward the model, there was no one there.

13 In the paragraph above, sentence 2 is out of order. Where should it BEST be placed?

A before sentence 1

B after sentence 3

C after sentence 4

D after sentence 5

Use the paragraph below to answer the question.

1 It keeps students from doing their best. **2** Laziness is an awful quality for students to have. **3** When lazy students have to work in a group, it hurts everyone in the group. **4** Lazy students disappoint parents and teachers. **5** Worst of all, most students who are lazy don't get far in life.

14 In the paragraph above, sentence 1 is out of order. Where should it BEST be placed?

A after sentence 2

B after sentence 3

C after sentence 4

D after sentence 5

Use the paragraph below to answer the question.

> **1** The idea of having to speak in front of a group is terrifying for some people. **2** Many people fear public speaking. **3** Some people fear it so fiercely that they get sweaty palms and shaky voices when forced to speak to a group. **4** Other people are so afraid to speak in public that they avoid it at all costs. **5** Public speaking is a challenging task for many people.

15 **In the paragraph above, sentence 2 is out of order. Where should it BEST be placed?**

A. before sentence 1

B. after sentence 3

C. before sentence 5

D. after sentence 5

For 16–20, read each paragraph and decide which closing sentence would be MOST appropriate.

16 **Which sentence would be the BEST closing sentence in the paragraph below?**

> Ernie was very tired. He had been up all night with his crying baby brother, Pedro. Pedro was teething and had only allowed Ernie to take a few light naps by the edge of the crib. Now, Ernie was groggy as he got dressed for school.

A Pedro should see the doctor today.

B Ernie's mom was very irresponsible.

C It was to be a long day for Ernie.

D Ernie wanted to cry and run away.

17 **Which sentence would be the BEST closing sentence in the paragraph below.**

> How much allowance should a twelve-year-old get? Some parents say that their kids should not get any allowance at all. Others think it is fair to have an allowance, and it should be given according to age. In that case, a twelve-year-old should get a twelve-dollar weekly allowance. Still other parents believe that twelve-year-olds should earn allowance based on how well they do chores.

A Allowance is a thing of the past.

B There are clearly many takes on how much allowance a twelve-year-old should receive.

C Ultimately, allowance amounts should be determined by the twelve-year-olds themselves.

D Allowance payment is up to the parent.

18 Which sentence would be the BEST closing sentence in the paragraph below?

Foster felt jealous. He was jealous of Teddy's new shoes and of Teddy's designer pencil pouch. It always seemed that Teddy had the best of everything. Now, Teddy was going to get to be the class president.

A Foster was in a bad mood.

B Foster was clearly not a good friend to Teddy.

C Foster felt more jealous now than ever.

D Teddy was better than Foster.

19 Which sentence would be the BEST closing sentence in the paragraph below?

The time crept away as evening on Willow Creek turned to a warm summer night. Connie and Earl sat quietly on Connie's back porch just taking in the beauty of the evening. They hadn't talked since Grandma's funeral, and now things seemed like the picture of peace.

A It was as if Grandma sent her comfort to them through the warm night air.

B Connie and Earl were hungry and tired.

C Earl decided it was time to go home; he had had enough peace and quiet for one day.

D Connie decided that now was a great time for dancing; she grabbed Earl and spun him around.

20 Which sentence would be the BEST closing sentence in the paragraph below?

There was nothing that Brian couldn't fix. He could repair it all. Last week, he had fixed Aunt Carla's watch. Yesterday, it was the icemaker on the fridge. What would Brian fix today?

A The dog looked like he had an injured leg, Brian thought.

B Brian's mom was tired of her son trying to fix everything.

C Brian needed to learn to buy new things instead of fixing old ones.

D He looked around the room for something that needed his magic touch.

Chapter 12
Using Resource Materials

This chapter addresses the following GPS-based CRCT standards:

ELA6W3	The student uses research and technology to support writing. The student
	a. Uses organizational features of electronic text (e.g., bulletin boards, databases, keyword searches, e-mail addresses) to locate relevant information.
	c. Cites references.

WHY RESEARCH?

We discussed creating paragraphs in chapter 11. But before you begin putting together paragraphs into a paper, it's important to **research**. Now, you might wonder why this is. It's good to research so you can know enough about your topic. Your readers need to be able to trust the things you write.

There are two basic ways to research. One is to use **printed sources**. This includes books from the library. It also means sources like newspapers, encyclopedias, and journals.

The other way to research is to use **electronic sources**. This means using the Internet. You probably already know how to IM your friends and watch videos online. It's also important to know how to use the Web for research.

ELECTRONIC RESEARCH SOURCES

The Web is the biggest resource for just about any type of information. This can be very good. Still, get permission from a parent, teacher, or guardian before you use the Web. Be sure that links you click on appear to be directly related to your research.

There are many parts of the Web. How can you know where to begin? Three key **electronic research sources** are **search engines**, **databases**, and **group communication**.

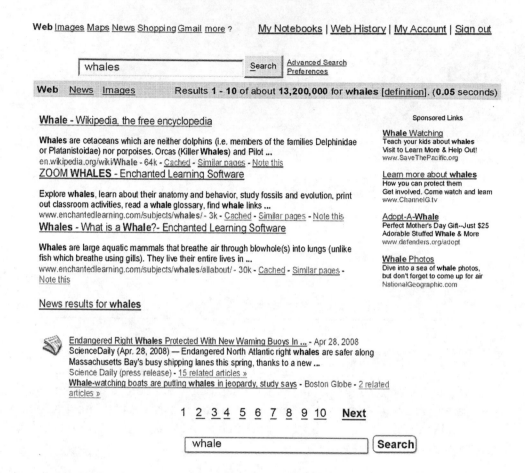

Web Images Maps News Shopping Gmail more ? My Notebooks | Web History | My Account | Sign out

whales   [Search]   Advanced Search / Preferences

Web News Images   Results **1 - 10** of about **13,200,000** for **whales** [definition]. **(0.05 seconds)**

Whale - Wikipedia, the free encyclopedia

Whales are cetaceans which are neither dolphins (i.e. members of the families Delphinidae or Platanistoidae) nor porpoises. Orcas (Killer **Whales**) and Pilot ...
en.wikipedia.org/wiki/Whale - 64k - Cached - Similar pages - Note this

ZOOM **WHALES** - Enchanted Learning Software

Explore **whales**, learn about their anatomy and behavior, study fossils and evolution, print out classroom activities, read a **whale** glossary, find **whale** links ...
www.enchantedlearning.com/subjects/whales/ - 3k - Cached - Similar pages - Note this

Whales - What is a **Whale**?- Enchanted Learning Software

Whales are large aquatic mammals that breathe air through blowhole(s) into lungs (unlike fish which breathe using gills). They live their entire lives in ...
www.enchantedlearning.com/subjects/whales/allabout/ - 30k - Cached - Similar pages - Note this

News results for **whales**

Endangered Right **Whales** Protected With New Warning Buoys In ... - Apr 28, 2008
ScienceDaily (Apr. 28, 2008) — Endangered North Atlantic right **whales** are safer along Massachusetts Bay's busy shipping lanes this spring, thanks to a new ...
Science Daily (press release) - 15 related articles »
Whale-watching boats are putting **whales** in jeopardy, study says - Boston Globe - 2 related articles »

Sponsored Links

Whale Watching
Teach your kids about **whales**
Visit to Learn More & Help Out!
www.SaveThePacific.org

Learn more about **whales**
How you can protect them
Get involved. Come watch and learn
www.ChannelG.tv

Adopt-A-**Whale**
Perfect Mother's Day Gift--Just $25
Adorable Stuffed **Whale** & More
www.defenders.org/adopt

Whale Photos
Dive into a sea of **whale** photos,
but don't forget to come up for air
NationalGeographic.com

1 2 3 4 5 6 7 8 9 10 **Next**

whale   [Search]

SEARCH ENGINES

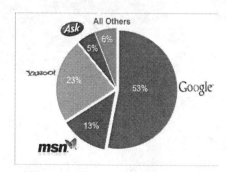

A **search engine** is the easiest way to find things on the Web. Google™ (http://www.google.com) is the most popular search engine. Yahoo!™ (http://www.yahoo.com) and Ask™ (http://www.ask.com) are also widely used. Different engines may give you different results. So if you don't find what you are looking for, try a different search engine.

To use a search engine, type a **keyword** into the search bar. Keywords are just what they sound like— key, or important, words. They are words that help you find relevant pages. They don't need to include proper capital letters or punctuation. They do need to be spelled correctly. You also don't need to put them into sentences or include very common words like *a*, *and*, or *the*. The best way to explain keywords is to use an example.

Let's say you are looking for facts about whales. Type *whales* into a search engine and press Enter (or click on the Search button in the search engine window). The engine delivers a list of links that have something to do with whales. Somewhere on the page, it tells you how many pages it has found. Did it turn up millions of results?

Web Images Maps News Shopping Gmail more ?   My Notebooks | Web History | My Account | Sign out

| whales | Search | Advanced Search |
Preferences

Web   News   Images   Results **1 - 10** of about **13,200,000** for **whales** [definition]. (**0.05** seconds)

Searches are designed to find pages that are of interest to you. Some pages will be full of facts. Other pages may not work. You can often tell by a page's title whether it is of value or not. Pages that appear to be from encyclopedias or biology sites should be good for this search. News, university, or government sites also tend to be factual. Some user-edited sites, like Wikipedia, often contain good information also. They may have errors, though. Check any facts that you use from user-edited sites. A blog (a kind of personal Web diary) may or may not be helpful. Likewise, clicking on an ad is not worth your time.

What if you want pages on only one kind of whale? Try searching *blue whales*. How many fewer pages does this search give you? Hundreds of thousands fewer? This is because it focused on pages with both words. However, it found pages that have both the word *blue* and the word *whale* in them. Some of these pages are not about blue whales; they just happen to have both words.

To make your search narrower, put quotation marks around your keywords. Search for *"blue whales"* and see how many pages come up. Look at how much better the first few results look. You can focus even more. Try *"blue whales" habitat arctic ocean*. This is very specific! It should now only list pages about whether blue whales live in this ocean or not.

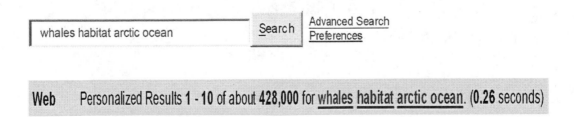

Keyword searches can become very detailed. It's a good idea to start out simple, just like we did with our whale search. You don't want to miss a good resource by being too specific right away. If you want more tips, look around your search engine's main page. There should be a link for more help.

When you find good pages, you should save them for later. To do this, use a tool called **bookmarks** or **favorites**. If you're at home, you can bookmark pages to your own computer. Look through the Help menu on your browser to find out how. If you are on someone else's computer, you should not create bookmarks for them. It's smart to use one of three methods:

- Write down links, which can take time

- E-mail links to yourself (we'll talk about e-mail later)

- Use an online bookmark site like del.icio.us, which stores all your links for free

The best way to learn more about search engines is to use them. With these simple tips, you should be able to find almost anything you need.

Practice 1: Search Engines
6W3a

1. To find facts about the world's fastest airplane, which keywords should you search FIRST?

   A. airplane speeds throughout world

   B. airplane highest ever rate of speed worldwide

   C. world's fastest airplane

   D. which airplane is the fastest in the world?

2. Which would be the LEAST helpful search for details about LeBron James's first year in the NBA?

   A. Lebron James first year in the NBA   C. Lebron James first year

   B. Lebron James first year NBA   D. Lebron James

3. After looking for poems by Emily Dickinson, the search engine gave Kerry these results. Which would be MOST likely to help her with her paper?

   A. Collected Poems of Emily Dickinson – Buy for $8.99

   B. Complete Online Archive of Emily Dickinson Poems

   C. "Why I love Emily Dickinson's Poems," by David Jones

   D. How Emily Dickinson's unusual life inspired her poems

DATABASES

Search engines are great most of the time. But sometimes you want sources that are more "serious." These are articles written by experts. They are usually found in college journals. Some are in magazines like *National Geographic* or *Popular Science*. A **database** is a collection of articles like these. They are written by people who have done a large amount of research about the topic you're searching for. The good news is that using a database is a lot like using a search engine.

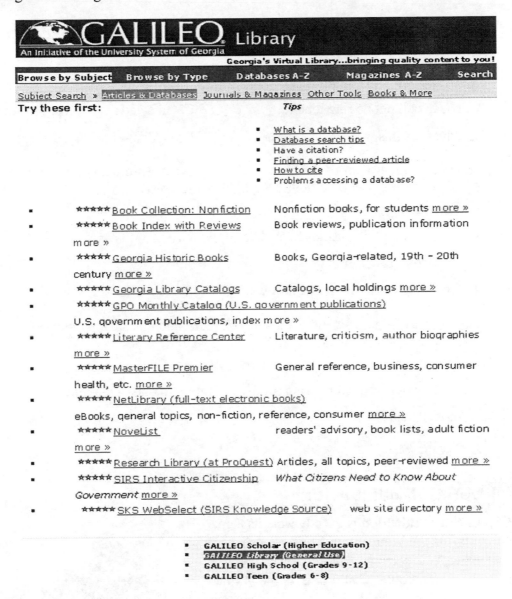

For starters, let's try the Google™ database. It's simpler than most, so it's a good way to learn. Go to http://www.scholar.google.com and search for *whales* again. Do you see how different this search looks? Most of the results probably have very long names with big words. Many of them are from colleges or research firms. It may take longer to find the best sources when using a database, but it can be worth the effort because experts wrote most of these. Some may even have brand new facts.

Databases should not have ads or links to user sites. Most of the time, any result in a database is suitable for a school paper. This doesn't mean each entry will be right for you. If you're looking for articles on blue whale habitats, don't settle for one on blue whale eating habits.

There are many databases on the Web. Your school or local public library may have one of its own. For most databases, you'll need to be given access. This means that you will need a user name and password. Check with a teacher or librarian for details.

Practice 2:   Databases
6W3a

1. Databases are NOT likely to be good sources of information on

    A. cheap cell phone ring tones.

    B. advances in space travel.

    C. the end of the Korean War.

    D. William Shakespeare's sonnets.

2. You want to learn about the history of the African American civil rights movement. Which of these would be the BEST link to click on?

    A. The History of the Women's Rights Movement

    B. People with Disabilities Seek Their Own Civil Rights Movement

    C. The Road to Civil Rights for the Black Community

    D. Civil Rights in Ancient Europe

3. You need to find an article comparing modern and classical painters. Which of these would probably be the BEST keywords to search?

    A. compare modern classical painters

    B. I need an article comparing modern painters to classical painters

    C. modern classical

    D. art history

GROUP COMMUNICATION

Group communication is exactly what its name suggests. On the Web, groups of people can talk with each other. Your school or class also may have message boards, online groups, chat rooms, or blogs where students can exchange ideas and submit questions. You may also have your teacher's e-mail address. This can be very useful.

Be careful if you are about to use a public chat room or message board. *Public*, in this case, would mean that it is open to people besides just your classmates. You'll often have no idea what kinds of posts you may find on a public board or who is posting them. Even if a board or room seems to talk about research, some users can get off topic. Some might post offensive material. So, it would be wise to ask a parent, teacher, or guardian about these sites before you use one of them.

There will usually be someone moderating, or "in charge of," a board or chat. Even if there isn't, you should still behave well. Discussing topics online can be valuable, but there are some standards expected of each user.

- Speak to every other user with respect.
- Don't post anything rude.
- Treat people as well as you'd want them to treat you in real life.

E-mail is for writing electronically to a person or several people. It works very much like writing a letter, in that you need to know the other person's address. This is usually something like *name@domain.com*. Write brief and clear e-mail, just like you would for any other piece of writing. For research needs, you could use e-mail to ask a friend if he or she has books you can borrow. Or you might want to ask your teacher for a good source for your project.

USING SOURCES

To include research in a paragraph, you need to put it in your own words or quote it. You also need a way to tell your readers the sources you used. To **cite sources** is to show readers where you found your information. This is also a way of giving credit to the original source. Taking credit for someone else's work is a form of cheating called **plagiarism**. The whole point of researching for a paper is to make sure your paper has good facts, and you want readers to be able to check those facts.

> *When it comes to citing sources and writing bibliographies, your school will probably have its own style and rules. These may vary from the examples we've listed. Ask your teacher for the preferred way to document sources.*

Let's say you want to use an idea you found in an encyclopedia. You found it in an entry about the Andes Mountains. Most writers would cite that source this way:

> The Andes is the world's longest mountain range, according to the Encyclopedia Britannica.

or this way:

> The Andes is the world's longest mountain range (Encyclopedia Britannica).

Whether you're using facts from an online or offline source, you must document everything. You need to show your readers where they could go to read the same research that you read. At the end of your paper, you'll have a list of all the sources that you cited. This list is called your **bibliography**. Here are examples of how a few kinds of texts would be documented:

DOCUMENTING A BOOK:

Twain, Mark. *Life on the Mississippi*. Penguin Classics, 1984.

NEWSPAPER ARTICLE:

Dart, Bob. 2008. Lawmaker says airline "re-regulation" an option. *Atlanta Journal-Constitution,* 10 April, national edition.

OFFLINE ENCYCLOPEDIA:

Rosenberger, Homer. "Washington Monument." The Encyclopedia Americana. International ed. 2005.

WEB ARTICLE:

Kanamori, Hiroo. "The energy release in great earthquakes." Journal of Geophysical Research Volume 82, (1977): p. 2981. 1 May 2008. <http://adsabs.harvard.edu/>.

There are many other kinds of texts that you may find yourself citing. These are just a few samples to give you an idea. Ask your teacher for hand outs or Web sites you can use to check your citations and bibliography.

CHAPTER 12 SUMMARY

Don't Forget!

Search engines are used to find things on the Web.

Keywords are words entered in search engines.

Databases are collections of scholarly articles.

Group communication includes message boards, group blogs, and chat rooms.

E-mail is used to send messages electronically to specific people.

To **cite sources** is to show readers where they can go to look at your research.

A **bibliography** is a list of your documented sources.

CHAPTER 12 REVIEW

6W3a

1 Janelle is researching the history of her home town. She is from Rome, Georgia. What should she type in a search engine?

   A Rome

   B Rome history

   C Rome Georgia

   D Rome Georgia history

2 Mike and Trent disagree about how hockey's offside rule works. They decide to find the right answer on Google™. Which result should they click on FIRST?

   A learn the basics of hockey rules

   B explaining football's offside rule

   C I hate hockey's offside rule

   D the offside rule (ice hockey)

3 Samir is writing about his favorite video game, *Guitar Hero*. He wants to mention when the game came out. Which keyword group would be LEAST useful?

   A Guitar Hero release date

   B when did Guitar Hero come out

   C Guitar Hero first available

   D Guitar Hero important information

4 Ritchie and Kiara are making a list of all the films starring Will Smith. Which of these links would likely help them the MOST?

   A NFL.com player profile: Will Smith, #91, New Orleans Saints

   B Will Smith biography at Yahoo!

   C International Movie Database—Will Smith

   D Will Smith music videos at Rhapsody.com

5 You're trying to decide whether solar power plants are better than wind power plants. Which of these databases should you look through to help you choose?

   A Energy Technology

   B Military Power

   C Weather Research

   D Plants & Gardening

6 Kendra heard her cousin was hired to work as a foley artist. She has no idea what that means. To find out, which keywords should she enter in a search engine?

    A Kendra's cousin's new job

    B foley artist

    C kinds of artists

    D foley

7 Reese is using a message board to discuss dinosaur fossils. Another user posts a question that Reese doesn't know the answer to. How could Reese BEST respond to this post?

    A use a search engine to find the answer

    B make a really smart guess

    C insult the other user

    D steer the conversation to a new topic

8 A friend e-mails you to ask for directions to Shaw Park. If you're not sure, which keywords should you use to find out?

    A Shaw Park

    B Shaw Park directions

    C Shaw Park directons

    D directions to the park

9 As you are studying at home for an English Language Arts test, you realize you have a question for your teacher. Your teacher's answer to your question may also help your fellow students prepare for the test. What would be the BEST way to get the information you need and also be of help to your classmates?

    A Send an e-mail to your teacher and forward the answer to your friends.

    B Post a question on your class's electronic bulletin board for your teacher to answer.

    C Look up the answer using an Internet search engine.

    D Try to make time to visit the library and use the database there to find your answer.

10 Deka has four sources for her paper on American gymnastics, but she only wants to use three. Which source is the LEAST relevant?

    A American gymnasts—Wikipedia

    B history of the ancient olympics

    C USA gymnastic home page

    D Gymnastics Magazine

Georgia 6th Grade CRCT in English Language Arts Practice Test 1

The purpose of this practice test is to measure your progress in reading and writing skills. This practice test is based on the GPS-based CRCT standards for English Language Arts and adheres to the sample question format provided by the Georgia Department of Education.

General Directions:

1 Read all directions carefully.

2 Read each question or sample. Then choose the best answer.

3 Choose only one answer for each question. If you change an answer, be sure to erase your original answer completely.

Note: The corresponding GPS standards listed beside each question have the prefix "ELA" removed to make the best use of space.

1 **Which word in the sentence is an abstract noun?**   6C1a.i

Poets often like to talk about beauty when they describe trees, animals, and mountains.

A Poets

B beauty

C trees

D mountains

2 **Which word in the sentence is a personal pronoun?**   6C1a.ii

Tracy has spotted quite a few redbirds in the backyard because she keeps a tray of seeds and fruits on the deck.

A Tracy

B few

C she

D tray

3 **Which word in the sentence is a proper adjective?**   6C1a.iii

Showing thoroughbred dogs, such as English bulldogs, in large stadiums has become a popular pastime.

A thoroughbred

B English

C large

D popular

4 **Which sentence below contains a transitive verb?**   6C1a.iv

A The teacher is very happy with the results of the spelling test.

B There were twenty entries in the computer division of the science fair.

C Reading science fiction is almost an obsession with my uncle.

D Good fences make good neighbors.

5 **Which word in the sentence is a helping verb?**   6C1a.v

The natives are very knowledgeable about herbs, and they have helped us with many medicines.

A are

B knowledgeable

C have

D helped

6 **Which word in the sentence is an adverb?**   6C1a.vi

We ran quickly to the pool and began the difficult test of swimming ten laps.

A ran   **C** difficult

B quickly   **D** ten

7 **Which word in the sentence should be capitalized?**   6C1f 6W2 6W4c

Jose was born twelve years ago at a downtown hospital in Atlanta, georgia.

A twelve

B downtown

C hospital

D georgia

8 Which word in the sentence is a coordinating conjunction? 6C1a.viii

Excellence and determination are hallmarks of a successful academic career.

A and

B are

C of

D a

9 Which word in the sentence should be capitalized? 6C1f 6W2 6W4c

The New York City marathon is a famous race that my mother is training for this summer.

A marathon

B race

C mother

D summer

10 What part of the sentence is the underlined word? 6C1b

Geographers organize <u>information</u> about each country of the world.

A subject

B verb

C direct object

D predicate noun

11 Which group of words below is a simple sentence? 6C1c

A Many different cultures exist in the United States, and each brings its own benefits to our society.

B The English language has many thousands of words from other languages.

C Although we may know a word comes from another language, we may not know its root meaning.

D Talking about words and learning new idioms.

12 What punctuation needs to be inserted in the sentence? 6C1c,d,f 6W2 6W4c

The northeastern United States has a dense population and that means many people live very closely together.

A a semicolon after *United States*

B a colon after *United States*

C a comma after *population*

D a semicolon after *population*

13 Which word in the sentence is misspelled? 6C1e,f 6W2 6W4c

There were over twenty babys in the hospital nursery.

A There

B twenty

C babys

D nursery

14 **What part of the sentence is the underlined word?** 6C1b

New Hampshire is a <u>state</u> in the northeast region of the United States.

A subject

B simple predicate

C direct object

D predicate noun

15 **What punctuation needs to be inserted in the sentence?** 6C1f 6W2 6W4c

Tyrone please bring your gym bag and books to the school office.

A a semicolon after *Tyrone*

B a comma after *Tyrone*

C a comma after *bag*

D a semicolon after *bag*

16 **A narrative paragraph does which of the following?** 6W1a,c 6W2

A It describes with vivid detail.

B It informs or explains something.

C It persuades the reader to a particular point of view.

D It tells a story.

Use the paragraph below to answer question 17.

Janna stopped her bike in front of the store. She padlocked the tire to the bike rack. She walked in and looked around. Right away, she saw some pretty picture frames. One of these will make a nice birthday gift for Tammy, she thought. She bought the frame, put it in her backpack, and started for home.

17 **Which organizational pattern does this passage use?** 6W1a,c 6W2

A chronological

B cause-effect

C compare/contrast

D question-answer

18 **Which word BEST fills the blank?** 6W1d 6W4b

Katie's Xbox can only play games. _____, my PS2 can play games and DVDs.

A Even though

B In addition

C However

D Because

Use the paragraph below to answer question 19.

1 The hunter trailed the lion. 2 The jungle path was thick. 3 He hunter could barely see ahead. 4 Then, he heard a low growl. 5 Afraid of the hungry lion, the villagers had hired the hunter. 6 He listened carefully and pointed his rifle in the direction of the sound. 7 He fired twice…and then he heard a roar and rustling that got farther and farther away. 8 The lion had escaped.

19 **Which sentence does not**   6W2b
relate to the rest of the   6W4b
**paragraph above and
should be removed?**

A   sentence 2   C   sentence 5

B   sentence 4   D   sentence 7

Use the paragraph below to answer question 20.

Cell phones are everywhere today. In the last twenty years, they have become something many people can afford and want to have. In some countries, there are more cell phones than there are people. In the United States, fifty percent of children have cell phones.

20 **Which sentence would be**   6W2
the BEST closing sentence   6W4b
in the paragraph?

A   Cell phones cannot be used in some places.

B   The first cell phone was invented in the 1940s.

C   Cell phones were once a luxury, but now it seems that none of us can live without them.

D   Not all cell phones get the same reception, which mostly depends on the service provider.

Use the paragraph below to answer question 21.

1 The Taíno Indians lived on islands in the Caribbean. 2 Although they no longer exist, the Taíno were an important tribe. 3 They invented a universal language. 4 They also were good sailors and fishermen. 5 After Spanish settlers came in 1508, the number of Taínos dropped due to disease and fighting the Spanish. 6 By 1544, there were only 60 Taínos remaining. 7 Soon, they were gone too.

21 **Which sentence is the topic**   6W2
**sentence of the above
paragraph?**

A   sentence 2

B   sentence 3

C   sentence 5

D   sentence 6

Use the paragraph below to answer question 22.

To let your parents know that you are ready for a pet, you need to show them. First, be sure to do the chores you have been given. Then, do something extra that you have not been asked to do. After demonstrating that you are responsible, you also have to tell them. Write down why you want a pet and what you would do to take care of it. It may not be easy, but if you are prepared, you will be convincing!

22 **Which sentence would make**   6W2
    the BEST topic sentence for
    this paragraph?

    A Deciding whether you want a pet is not always the easiest thing to do.

    B It takes planning and logic to convince your parents that you can take care of a pet.

    C Before you get a pet, be sure to consider how your life will change once it is in the house.

    D A pet takes lots of time and attention, so you need to make a real commitment.

Use the paragraph below to answer question 23.

Having a model railroad can be really fun. Some people like true models. This means they have a scale model that looks like a real-life railroad in miniature. Others have toy trains that run on a layout they create from imagination. There can be made-up towns, hills, rivers, and so on. Either way, it's exciting to build a track, add all the scenery, and then watch the train run through it.

23 **What is the main idea of this**   6W2
    paragraph?

    A Model railroading is a fun hobby.

    B Model trains are better than toy trains.

    C True models need to be scale replicas.

    D Adding scenery is the most fun part.

Use the paragraph below to answer question 24.

1 Have you ever heard of busking? 2 The first time you hear that term, it might sound like some strange kind of transportation. 3 In America, we still usually call someone playing on the street a street musician. 4 It's a British term that refers to performing on the street, like musicians who set up at a park or jugglers who perform near a bus station. 5 A busker can be almost any kind of performance artist. 6 But if you're in London and see someone playing a guitar in the Tube, that's a busker!

24 In the paragraph above, sentence 3 is out of order. Where should it BEST be placed?   6W2 6W4b

   A after sentence 1

   B after sentence 4

   C after sentence 5

   D after sentence 6

Use the paragraph below to answer question 25.

1 My cousin Jimmy has asthma. 2 It's a condition that can't really be cured, just controlled. 3 He has to carry an inhaler, and he visits the doctor often. 4 His asthma makes it hard to breathe. 5 Last year, I thought I had asthma too, but Aunt Laureen said I was just feeling for Jimmy. 6 He told me once what happens: the airways in his lungs swell up, and the air can't get in or out. 7 Jimmy has to be careful not to play or run too hard, and he has to stay inside during the worst parts of allergy season.

25 Which sentence does not relate to the rest of the paragraph above and should be removed?   6W2 6W4b

   A sentence 1

   B sentence 3

   C sentence 5

   D sentence 7

Use the paragraph below to answer question 26.

In science class, we made a rainbow. The teacher gave us all a dish of water. Then, we put a small mirror in the dish, held up against one side by a glob of clay. Next, we shined a flashlight on the part of the mirror that was under the water. Finally, we held a piece of white paper where the mirror reflected the light.

26 Which sentence would be the BEST closing sentence in the paragraph? 6W2 6W4b

A We had to hold the flashlight steady.

B. One person held the paper, while the other held the flashlight.

C. We had to pass around the flash-lights because there weren't enough for everyone.

D. There, on the paper, a rainbow appeared.

27 On which Web site would you MOST LIKELY find the results of the Super Bowl? 6W3a

A www.georgia.gov

B www.nationalgeographic.com

C www.usa.gov

D www.msn.com

28 Which word in the sentence is a collective noun? 6C1a

It's getting to be that time of year when our class has its annual field day.

A time

B year

C class

D annual

29 Which word in the sentence is a reflexive pronoun? 6C1a.ii

Many people are surprised when they catch a glimpse of themselves in a mirror.

A Many

B people

C they

D themselves

30 Which sentence below contains a demonstrative adjective? 6C1a.iii

A I love to look for shells as I walk along the beach.

B Many people have found jewelry by using a metal detector on the beach.

C Others have found aged beach wood that has floated from shipwrecks.

D Those rare stones were found by a treasure hunter.

31 Which sentence below contains an intransitive verb? 6C1a.iv

A Every morning I run down the street to the park and then back again.

B Alexandra plays the piano in her spare time.

C My mother takes all our photographs and puts them in scrapbooks.

D Wow! The Atlanta Falcons won the game!

32 **Which word in the sentence is the object of the preposition?** 6C1a.vii

Alyssa paints beautiful flowers with the watercolors that her grandparents sent her.

A flowers

B with

C watercolors

D grandparents

33 **Which word in the sentence is a subordinating conjunction?** 6C1a.viii

What do you think of most when you go to a new state?

A What

B most

C when

D to

34 **Which word in the sentence is a predicate adjective?** 6C1b

Reading books about imaginary worlds is fun.

A Reading

B books

C worlds

D fun

35 **Which group of words below is a compound sentence?** 6C1c

A People speaking English, French, Chinese, Italian, and Portuguese.

B When tourists go to Toronto, they find many different cultures.

C Many TV stations broadcast in as many as thirty different languages.

D People come with one language, and they learn many others.

36 **Which word in the sentence is misspelled?** 6C1e,f
6W2
6W4c

Because of the circumstances, the teacher was extremely embarassed.

A Because

B circumstances

C extremely

D embarassed

37 **Where should commas be placed in the sentence below?** 6C1f
6W2
6W4c

On February 1 1851 the city of Portland was incorporated.

A after *February 1* and *1851*

B after *February 1* and *Portland*

C after *1851* and *Portland*

D after *of* and *Portland*

38 Where should the comma be placed in the sentence below? 6C1f 6W2 6W4c

Olympic runners usually have long legs strong muscles, and great determination.

A after *runners*

B after *usually*

C after *long*

D after *legs*

39 What word in the sentence should be capitalized? 6C1f 6W2 6W4c

My grandfather told me that Labor Day is a national holiday that takes place on the first monday of every September.

A grandfather

B national

C holiday

D monday

Read this passage. Then answer question 40.

1 Jamie called Rico "shorty." 2 That wasn't very nice, and it didn't really make sense. 3 Rico can't help that he's not very tall.

40 Which transition BEST fits before sentence 3? 6W1d 6W4b

A Since

B After all,

C In the meantime,

D For the reason that

Read this passage, and then answer question 41.

1 The moon revolves around earth, orbiting our planet every 27 1/3 days. 2 This period is known as a sidereal month. 3 It takes 29 1/2 days for the moon to complete its cycle of phases. 4 This is called the synodic, or lunar, month.

41 Which transition BEST fits before sentence 3? 6W1d 6W4b

A Otherwise,

B Even though,

C On the other hand,

D As a result of this,

Use the paragraph below to answer question 42.

1 Daylight saving time (DST) means turning the clocks ahead so that the afternoons are longer. 2 Clocks are turned ahead one hour near the start of spring; then they are turned back in fall. 3 Some people think Benjamin Franklin invented Modern DST. 4 This is probably because he always said, "Early to bed, and early to rise, makes a man healthy, wealthy and wise." 5 But it was actually proposed by builder William Willett in 1907. 6 Willett loved to play golf, and he hated cutting his game short in the evenings.

42 Which sentence does not relate to the rest of the paragraph above and should be removed? 6W2 6W4b

A sentence 2

B sentence 3

C sentence 5

D sentence 6

Use the paragraph below to answer question 43.

1 In 1732, James Edward Oglethorpe received the charter for a new colony. **2** He chose 116 pioneers to sail to the coast. **3** They set up camp where we now find Savannah. **4** He built forts around the colony. **5** The first six years were hard, but in time the colony prospered. **6** Georgia became an important battleground during the American Revolution. **7** Georgia was the last of the original thirteen colonies.

43 In the paragraph above, sentence 7 is out of order. Where should it BEST be placed? 6W2 6W4b

A   before sentence 1

B   after sentence 2

C   after sentence 4

D   after sentence 5

Use the paragraph below to answer question 44.

Sound is a kind of energy created by vibration. Anything can vibrate—solids, liquids, even gases. Vibrations travel in waves through any of these media. Sound cannot be made in a vacuum or in outer space, where there is nothing to vibrate.

44 Which transition BEST fits before sentence 4? 6W1d 6W4b

A   Consequently,

B   That is,

C   Although,

D   Still,

Use the paragraph below to answer question 45.

1 I just hate to get up and talk in front of class. **2** Even if I feel prepared, it's never easy. **3** I stand there, all alone, with everyone staring at me. **4** My hands get clammy, and my mouth dries up. **5** Who can talk when that happens! **6** It can be frightening to give an oral report.

45 Which sentence is the topic sentence of the above paragraph? 6W2

A   sentence 1

B   sentence 3

C   sentence 5

D   sentence 6

Use the paragraph below to answer question 46.

There are some museums that display art. They are great places to learn about artists and history. Other museums feature science and technology. Still others are dedicated to the history of the world. They have big skeletons of dinosaurs and dioramas of ancient cultures. Being in a museum really makes you think.

46 Which sentence would make the BEST topic sentence for this paragraph? 6W2

A   There are many different kinds of museums in the world.

B   Many people don't like going to museums.

C   Museums are great places to learn about the world.

D   Our class took a trip to a museum of natural history.

Use the paragraph below to answer question 47.

Some day, we might not have to drive, but it won't be because we have no cars. Scientists are working on a driverless car. The car would have special sensors to "see" the road and all obstacles. It would, of course, have a special navigation system. There are many questions that need to be answered, but some companies are already working on prototypes.

47 **What is the main idea of this paragraph?** 6W2

A Could a driverless car ever really be safe?

B A driverless car is like a taxi, without the cab driver.

C Cars don't really need drivers.

D Cars that don't need drivers are being developed.

Use the paragraph below to answer question 48.

1 Today, ballroom dancing has new status. **2** Ballroom dancing used to be something kids were forced to do by their parents. **3** Classes taught young people dances for formal events. **4** Most kids didn't like it, and many didn't attend the kind of parties where they would use it. **5** Young people are learning formal dances more than ever. **6** Thanks to movies like *Strictly Ballroom* and *Dance with Me* and shows like "Dancing with the Stars," there are now popular role models for ballroom dancing.

48 **In the paragraph above, sentence 1 is out of order. Where should it BEST be placed?** 6W2 6W4b

A after sentence 2

B after sentence 3

C after sentence 4

D after sentence 5

Use the paragraph below to answer question 49.

My dad is teaching me to play chess. It's not an easy game. Some people think it's boring, especially if they are used to video games. But once you know more about it, you see that it takes a lot of brain power. The key to winning is to see ahead. A good chess player has to figure out what his opponent might do in the next few moves.

49 Which sentence would be the BEST closing sentence in the paragraph?   6W2
6W4b

A The history of chess is very interesting.

B Chess pieces are based on divisions of the military.

C Seeing what your opponent might do helps you choose the right moves to make.

D For my birthday, Dad got me a chess set where the pieces are Star Wars characters.

50 Which word in the sentence is a possessive noun?   6C1a.i

The major league baseball team that has won the most consecutive divisional titles is Atlanta's own Braves.

A team

B title

C Atlanta's

D Braves

51 Which word in the sentence is an indefinite pronoun?   6C1a.ii

"Would someone come in here and help me with dinner?" Mom asked.

A Would

B someone

C me

D Mom

52 Which word in the sentence is a linking verb?   6C1a.iv

The girls were working and cleaning their rooms, but they looked happy doing it.

A working

B cleaning

C looked

D doing

53 Which word in the sentence is a predicate adjective?   6C1b

Africa's Sahara Desert is larger than all the land in the United States.

A Sahara

B larger

C all

D land

54 Which word in the sentence is misspelled?   6C1e,f
6W2
6W4c

My favorite desert is chocolate-covered brownies with ice cream on top.

A favorite

B desert

C chocolate

D brownies

55 **What punctuation needs to be inserted in the sentence?** 6C1c,d,f 6W2 6W4c

When neighbors live together peacefully the city is known as a friendly place.

A a period after *peacefully*

B a comma after *peacefully*

C a semicolon after *peacefully*

D quotation marks around *peacefully*

56 **Where should the question mark go in the sentence?** 6C1f 6W2 6W4c

Sean did not hear his father say, "Are you ready yet"

A after *Sean*

B after *say*

C after *ready*

D after *yet*

57 **Which word in the sentence is a preposition?** 6C1avii 6W2

The cherry blossom trees bloom in the spring, and their beauty captivates many fans.

A blooms

B in

C their

D many

58 **What part of speech is the underlined word in the sentence?** 6C1a.ix 6W2

<u>Wow</u>! Did you know that there is a valley in east Africa that is 4,000 miles long?

A noun

B verb

C conjunction

D interjection

59 **What punctuation needs to be inserted in the sentence?** 6C1c,d,f 6W2 6W4c

The "money capital" of the United States New York City has a large population of bankers.

A a comma after *capital*

B comma after *United States* and *New York City*

C a semicolon after *United States*

D commas after *capital* and *United States*

60 **Which word in the sentence is a common adjective?** 6C1a.iii 6W2

Kyle is most happy when he is playing with toy trains.

A Kyle

B most

C toy

D trains

Georgia 6th Grade CRCT in English Language Arts Practice Test 2

The purpose of this practice test is to measure your progress in reading and writing skills. This practice test is based on the GPS-based CRCT standards for English Language Arts and adheres to the sample question format provided by the Georgia Department of Education.

General Directions:

1 Read all directions carefully.

2 Read each question or sample. Then choose the best answer.

3 Choose only one answer for each question. If you change an answer, be sure to erase your original answer completely.

Note: The corresponding GPS standards listed beside each question have the prefix "ELA" removed to make the best use of space.

1 **Which word in the sentence is an abstract noun?**   6C1a.i

Everyone could feel the excitement in the room as the party began.

A Everyone

B feel

C excitement

D room

2 **What type of pronoun is the underlined word?**   6C1a.ii

A mineral such as bauxite can have something profitable produced from it.

A personal pronoun

B possessive pronoun

C demonstrative pronoun

D indefinite pronoun

3 **What word in the sentence is a demonstrative adjective?**   6C1a.iii

Apples, grapes, melons, peanuts, and onions are grown in the South, and these crops are very important to the South's economy.

A peanuts

B onions

C these

D South's

4 **What type of verb is the group of underline words?**   6C1a.iv

Oranges, tangerines, grapefruits, and limes are grown in Florida.

A linking verb

B helping verb

C intransitive verb

D transitive verb

5 **Which word in the sentence is a helping verb?**   6C1a.v

Many tourists to Mississippi have enjoyed riding on the river steamboats.

A tourists

B have

C enjoyed

D riding

6 **Which word in the sentence is an adverb?**   6C1a.vi

The Midwest is known for its farming, but the number of small farms has fallen sharply.

A known   C small

B farming   D sharply

7 **Which word in the sentence is the object of a preposition?**   6C1a.vii

Chicago is a large and important city in the Midwest.

A large

B city

C in

D Midwest

8 **Which group of words in the sentence is a correlative conjunction?**   6C1a.viii

Both natural resources and an inviting climate draw many people to the West every year.

A Both…and

B natural…inviting

C resources…climate

D and…to

9 **What part of speech is the underlined word in the sentence?** 6C1a.ix

<u>Oh</u>! The view from the top of the Grand Canyon in Arizona is spectacular.

A adjective

B pronoun

C adverb

D interjection

10 **Which word in the sentence is the direct object of the sentence?** 6C1b

Early western settlers moving from the East used wagons called prairie schooners.

A western

B settlers

C wagons

D prairie

11 **What is the group of words below?** 6C1c

Montreal, the capital of Quebec, is known around the world for its French heritage.

A simple sentence

B compound sentence

C complex sentence

D sentence fragment

12 **Which of the sentences below is punctuated correctly?** 6W4c,d,f 6W2

A Mauna Kea is an extinct volcano and it is the highest peak in all of Hawaii.

B Mauna Kea is an extinct volcano; and it is the highest peak in all of Hawaii.

C Mauna Kea is an extinct volcano: and it is the highest peak in all of Hawaii.

D Mauna Kea is an extinct volcano, and it is the highest peak in all of Hawaii.

13 **How can the sentence below be corrected?** 6C1e,f 6W2 6W4c

How many white-tailed deers did you see at the zoo?

A change *many* to *much*

B change *deers* to *deer*

C change *see* to *sea*

D change *zoo* to *Zoo*

14 **What would be the correct capitalization for the ending of the letter below?** 6C1f 6W2 6W4c

Dear Marie,

Thank you so much for the shirt you gave to me for my birthday. I'm planning on wearing it to your party this weekend.

sincerely yours,

Rebecca

A capitalize *sincerely* and *yours*

B capitalize *sincerely*

C capitalize *yours*

D do not capitalize any words at all

15 **How can the sentence below be corrected?** 6C1e,f 6W2 6W4c

The mechanic gave me some good advise when he said to trade in my car.

A   change the *mechanic* to *mechanick*

B   change *gave* to *given*

C   change *advise* to *advice*

D   change *said* to *told*

Use the paragraph below to answer question 16.

Our newest game, "The Galaxy and Beyond," is fun and educational! You can learn about planets and explore space while having an exciting adventure. The enjoyment never stops. Other games may be fun for a while, but they have limited endings. Someone wins, and others lose. Not so with "The Galaxy and Beyond"! You can play over and over and always have a new adventure.

16 **Which organizational pattern does this passage use?** 6W1a,c 6W2

A   chronological

B   cause-effect

C   effect-cause

D   compare/contrast

17 **If you want to write about how receiving a fifty States Commemorative Coin Program map got you started on collecting coins. Which organizational pattern would BEST work for this kind of story?** 6W1a,c 6W2

A   chronological

B   cause-effect

C   compare/contrast

D   question-answer

18 **Which word BEST fills the blank in this sentence?** 6W1d 6W4b

Our city is building bike paths to get people riding instead of driving. _____, they hope to cut down on smog and help people save gas.

A   In any case

B   Because

C   In this way

D   However

Use the paragraph below to answer question 19.

1 *The Simpsons* is one of the funniest shows on TV. **2** The family may not be the best people: Homer is not very smart; Marge lives in a fantasy world; Bart is a smart-mouthed delinquent; Lisa is an annoying braniac. **3** But, they are really comical characters. **4** I have Bart Simpson wallpaper on my computer. **5** The situations they get into are side-splitting. **6** The best thing is the spoof episodes, in which they live through a scenario from a movie. **7** For example, "You Only Move Twice" was done like a James Bond movie. **8** The guest star voices are a great addition.

19 **Which sentence does not relate to the rest of the paragraph above and should be removed?** 6W2 6W4b

A   sentence 2

B   sentence 4

C   sentence 6

D   sentence 7

Use the paragraph below to answer question 20.

The famous scientist Marie Curie was born in Poland. She moved to Paris to study. There, she met and married her husband Pierre. She became a pioneer in the study of radioactivity. She is the only person ever to win a Nobel Prize in two fields: chemistry and physics. Curie also was the first female professor at the University of Paris.

20 Which sentence would be the BEST closing sentence in the paragraph? 6W2 6W4b

A Probably the most famous female scientist, Madame Curie has inspired many people.

B Three radioactive minerals are named after the Curies.

C Madame Curie probably died of radiation poisoning because of her close work with radioactive materials.

D Several movies have been made about Madame Curie's life.

Use the paragraph below to answer question 21.

Austin and his family went to Yosemite National Park on their summer vacation. First, they traveled through many states. Then they entered the park and saw the Old Faithful geyser. After that, they went hiking along one of the nearby rivers. They ended the day with a camping trip into the woods.

21 What is the main idea of the paragraph? 6W2

A the games that Austin's family plays

B the Old Faithful geyser

C the fish in the nearby river

D Austin's family vacation

Use the paragraph below to answer question 22.

Who would have thought? Mom always says, "Take your vitamins," but I read that too many can be toxic. There is such a thing as vitamin poisoning. For example, too much Vitamin A can cause things like liver problems and hair loss. Too much Vitamin D can cause dehydration, vomiting, and other problems. But you would have to take a whole bottle a day of these vitamins for these things to happen. In the right doses, vitamins help you get the nutrition your body needs. So, Mom is right, and I can't get out of taking my daily vitamin!

22 **Which sentence would make the BEST topic sentence for this paragraph?**   6W2

A   People who take vitamins need to ask their doctor if they should stop.

B   I think my family takes too many vitamins.

C   It's good to take vitamins, but taking too many can be bad for you.

D   When you take vitamins, you can avoid serious illness.

Use the paragraph below to answer question 23.

An aqueduct is a man-made channel that carries water from one place to another. Aqueducts were invented in the Near East. The Egyptians and the Harappans used them to bring water to crops. The most famous aqueducts were built by the Romans in the 7th century B.C.E. Many still stand today, and some are still used. They were built in all parts of the Roman Empire, from Germany to Africa. Their engineering was so amazing that there was no better system for more than a thousand years.

23 **What is the main idea of this paragraph?**   6W2

A   Aqueducts are still used today.

B   Aqueducts have a rich history.

C   No one uses aqueducts anymore.

D   The Romans invented aqueducts.

Use the paragraph below to answer question 24.

For many immigrants, the first sight they see of the United States is the Statue of Liberty. The tall statue with her lamp raised high seems like a welcoming invitation to them. There are also welcoming words engraved at the base of the statue. Many of the immigrants come from countries with harsh politics. Finally, there are friendly officials who give them information and helpful advice as they enter the new country.

24 Which of the sentences in the paragraphshould NOT have been included? 6W2 6W4b

A For many immigrants, the first sight they see of the United States is the Statue of Liberty.

B The tall statue with her lamp raised high seems like a welcoming invitation to them.

C There are also welcoming words engraved at the base of the statue.

D Many of the immigrants come from countries with harsh politics.

Use the paragraph below to answer question 25.

1 When I grow up, I'd like to be a cryptanalyst. **2** That's someone who studies and deciphers hidden messages. **3** I really like games containing puzzles and secret messages that have to be solved. **4** Cryptography was first invented in ancient times. **5** It slowed down a person who was trying to read someone else's writing. **6** Today, it is very complex. **7** With computers and new theories, possible ciphers are endless. **8** I think this would be a fascinating job.

25 Which sentence does not relate to the rest of the paragraph above and should be removed? 6W2 6W4b

A sentence 1   C sentence 6

B sentence 3   D sentence 8

Use the paragraph below to answer question 26.

Courtney and Victoria chose Texas as the topic of their geography project. First, they decided what topics they would research. Then they went to the library and researched those topics.

26 Which of the following sentences would be the BEST choice for a closing sentence? 6W2

A They did a very good job.

B The library was close to their homes.

C Some of their friends liked their report.

D Finally, they typed all the information they had found into one report.

27 Brandon is using the   6W3a
Internet to do a search for a
project. Which of the following
keywords would BEST link him to
the prices of current Apple®
computers?

A computers

B business

C technology information

D Apple® website

28 What part of speech is the   6C1a.iii
underlined word?

Georgia is my favorite state because it has
all kinds of <u>wonderful</u> trees and flowers.

A noun

B adjective

C adverb

D interjection

29 What type of pronoun is the   6C1a.ii
underlined word?

Thoreau, the author of *Walden*, lived
alone in the woods and took care of
<u>himself</u> for two years.

A personal pronoun

B possessive pronoun

C demonstrative pronoun

D reflexive pronoun

30 What type of verb is the   6C1a.iv
group of underlined words?

Farming <u>has</u> always <u>been</u> an important
part of the South's culture and economy.

A linking verb

B action verb

C helping verb

D transitive verb

31 Which word in the   6C1a.vii
sentence is the
prepositional phrase modifying?

Detroit is the headquarters for the
American automobile industry.

A Detroit

B headquarters

C automobile

D industry

32 What word in the sentence   6C1a.viii
is a subordinating
conjunction?

If its antennas are included as part of the
total height of the Sears Tower, it is the
tallest building in the world.

A If   C in

B height   D of

33 Which word in the sentence   6C1b
is the predicate noun of the   6W2
sentence?   6W4c

"Bowash" is a name given to the chain of
cities from Boston to New York to
Washington, D.C.

A name

B chain

C cities

D Boston

34 Which word in the sentence   6C1a.i
is a plural noun?

Are children allowed to be in the
reception area of the hospital?

A children

B reception

C area

D hospital

35 **What part of speech is the underlined word?**   6C1a.iii

The city of Atlanta hosted the <u>famous</u> Olympic games in 1996.

A demonstrative pronoun

B proper adjective

C common noun

D common adjective

36 **What type of sentence is the sentence below?**   6C1c

Our family first visited the famous Niagara Falls, and then we went to Toronto, the capital of Ontario.

A simple

B compound

C complex

D compound-complex

37 **Which of the sentences below is punctuated correctly?**   6C1c,d,f 6W2 6W4c

A Although a plateau has at least one side with a steep slope, it is a large, mostly flat area of land.

B Although a plateau has at least one side with a steep slope: it is a large, mostly flat area of land.

C Although a plateau has at least one side with a steep slope, it is a large mostly flat area of land.

D Although a plateau has at least one side with a steep slope; it is a large, mostly flat area of land.

38 **What would be the correct capitalization for the sentence below?**   6C1f 6W2 6W4c

"The game show is about to begin!" said Jesse. "the last one here is a rotten egg!"

A capitalize *game*

B capitalize *show*

C capitalize *the* (after *Jesse*)

D capitalize *egg*

39 **Which words in the sentence need to have commas after them?**   6C1c,d,f 6W2 6W4c

Australia a continent in the southern hemisphere is located just south of New Guinea.

A *Australia* and *continent*

B *Australia* and *hemisphere*

C *continent* and *hemisphere*

D *hemisphere* and *south*

40 **Which word BEST fills the blank in this sentence?**   6W1d 6W4b

After you turn left at the corner, go straight for one block, and _____ turn right onto Mulroney Street.

A then

B next

C as well

D also

Read this passage. Then, answer question 41.

1 We were all eating lunch in the cafeteria. 2 Everyone was just talking and slurping, as usual. 3 The new kid jumped up on a table and started singing a song from *High School Musical*. 4 We stared with our mouths open, figuring he must have taken a dare.

41 Which transition BEST fits before sentence 3?

6W1d
6W4b

A Afterwards,

B Throughout,

C Today,

D Suddenly,

Use the paragraph below to answer question 42.

1 What can we learn from early American history? 2 History shows us how people from England came here so they could worship as they wished. 3 In this new land, they had that freedom, and they had a thanksgiving feast to celebrate. 4 That's the origin of the holiday called Thanksgiving. 5 History also shows why the northeast states are called New England. 6 This was the site of the original English colonies. 7 If you ever go to New England, be sure to see Jamestown, Virginia, for great historical attractions.

42 Which sentence does not relate to the rest of the paragraph above and should be removed?

6W2
6W4b

A sentence 1

B sentence 3

C sentence 5

D sentence 7

Use the paragraph below to answer question 43.

1 Everyone seems to be "going green" these days. 2 There are green cars, green cleaning products, and green energy, just to mention a few. 3 What does that mean? 4 Will everything be painted green? 5 One example is hybrid cars, which use less gasoline to save fossil fuel resources and pollute less. 6 Actually, it means that people and companies are making changes that will help to protect the environment.

43 In the paragraph above, sentence 6 is out of order. Where should it BEST be placed?

6W2
6W4b

A after sentence 1

B after sentence 2

C after sentence 3

D after sentence 4

Read this passage. Then answer question 44.

1 A recent news article reported that kids are using text messaging more than e-mail. 2 _____ e-mail is still used for formal purposes, kids now prefer to text when communicating with friends. 3 Texting is much more convenient because you can do it on the go. 4 The texting trend is relatively recent, but it seems to be here to stay.

44 Which transition BEST fits before sentence 2?

6W1d
6W4b

A Because

B Even though

C When

D Since

Use the paragraph below to answer question 45.

1 Marsupials are animals that have pouches. **2** The females carry their babies in the pouches. **3** Most people know that kangaroos are marsupials. **4** There are many marsupials all over the world. **5** They include koalas, wombats, gliders, opossums, and more. **6** Many today live in Australia. **7** But scientists believe marsupials originated in North America.

45 **Which sentence is the topic sentence of the above paragraph?**   6W2

A   sentence 2   C   sentence 5

B   sentence 4   D   sentence 7

Use the paragraph below to answer question 46.

When I get home, I first have to walk the dog. Molly is home alone all afternoon, so I take her for a nice long walk at the park down the street. When Molly and I get back, I grab a snack and do my homework. She always begs, even though she doesn't eat the fruit I usually munch on. When I'm done, I sometimes go watch TV. But by then, Mom normally gets home, so we talk about our day instead.

46 **Which sentence would make the BEST topic sentence for this paragraph?**   6W2

A   I have a set routine every day after school.

B   My dog is my best friend in the world.

C   TV keeps me company when I get home from school.

D   I don't like it that my mom has to work.

Use the paragraph below to answer question 47.

A civil war is very difficult because neighbors fight each other. What the parties fight about varies. Sometimes it is a government policy, as slavery was in America's Civil War. Other times, people fight over the use of land. They may also fight about certain religious rights. Usually, one group wants things to stay as they are, while the other wants them to change.

47 **What is the main idea of this paragraph?**   6W2

A   Civil wars are the same as other kinds of wars.

B   A civil war happens when people in the same culture or country fight over an issue.

C   The American Civil War led to slavery being stopped.

D   To learn about the why people fight over things, study the American Civil War.

Use the paragraph below to answer question 48.

1 I baked a batch of cookies this weekend. 2 They turned out well, and we all enjoyed eating them. 3 The hardest part was measuring all the ingredients correctly. 4 I was confused when the recipe said to add a pinch of salt. 5 How much is a pinch? 6 Once the ingredients were together, though, mixing was easy. 7 It was satisfying to drop the dough onto the cookie sheet and then watch the cookies brown in the oven!

48 In the paragraph above, sentence 2 is out of order. Where should it BEST be placed?   6W2   6W4b

A   before sentence 1

B   after sentence 3

C   after sentence 5

D   after sentence 7

Use the paragraph below to answer question 49.

The emperor penguin is the biggest of all penguins. emperor penguins live in Antarctica. Like all penguins, they can't fly. They eat fish, shrimp, and squid. They can hold their breath under water for almost twenty minutes.

49 Which sentence would be the BEST closing sentence in the paragraph?   6W2   6W4b

A   They have white feathers on their bellies, black feathers on their backs, and patches of yellow around their ears.

B   Emperor penguins are best known for the long trip they make each year to mate and raise their babies.

C   They usually live to be about twenty years old in the wild, but they can live to about fifty.

D   Like all penguins, emperor penguins are streamlined so they can swim faster.

50 What type of pronoun is the underlined word?   6C1a.ii

Not just <u>anyone</u> can do the extensive metalwork required for building skyscrapers.

A   personal pronoun

B   possessive pronoun

C   demonstrative pronoun

D   indefinite pronoun

51 Which word in these sentences is a state-of-being verb?   6C1a.iv

The young man eagerly addressed the classroom, "Good morning. I am Ryan Thomas, your new social studies teacher."

A eagerly

B addressed

C am

D your

52 What is the group of words below?   6C1c

       Back in the "Wild West" days, people in the East would pack up all their belongings and strike out on wilderness roads to find new land and fortune, they were hoping to have their dreams fulfilled by finding a new place to live.

A simple sentence

B sentence fragment

C complex sentence

D run-on sentence

53 How can the sentence below be corrected?   6C1e,f 6W2 6W4c

There were over a hundred floweres in the botanical garden.

A change the *There* to *Their*

B change the *hundred* to *hunderd*

C change the *floweres* to *flowers*

D change the *garden* to *gardin*

54 Which word in the sentence needs to have a comma after it?   6C1f 6W2 6W4c

Have you ever been to the continent of Europe Joaquin?

A you

B been

C continent

D Europe

55 What is the group of words below?   6C1c

While we were waiting to ride in *The Lady of the Mist*, we saw a beautiful rainbow over Niagara Falls.

A simple sentence

B compound sentence

C complex sentence

D sentence fragment

56 How should the sentence below be corrected?   6C1f 6W2 6W4c

Would you please pick up the phone.

A add a comma after *you*

B change *Would* to *Could*

C capitalize *you*

D change the period to a question mark

57 **Which word in the sentence is the predicate adjective?**   6C1b

The California Gold Rush was important to the development of the state of California.

A California

B Gold

C important

D development

58 **How should the sentence below be corrected?**   6C1f
6W2
6W4c

Although Kansas is a key farming state only ten percent of its citizens are farmers.

A add a comma after *Although*

B add a comma after *state*

C add a comma after *only*

D change *are* to *is*

59 **Which word in the sentence is the subject?**   6C1b

National forests protect many of our natural resources from being destroyed.

A National

B forests

C protect

D many

60 **Which word in the sentence is a collective noun?**   6C1a.i

Our family gets together every year at Vogel State Park to swim, hike, and eat.

A Our

B family

C together

D year